Sports Action

Riding

Sports Action

Riding

Edited by
Jane Holderness Roddam and
Helena Charlesworth

OCTOPUS BOOKS

Acknowledgements
Photographs:
Front jacket: Sporting Pictures (UK) Ltd
All photographs supplied by Jürgen Kemmler except for the following:
Barnaby's: 110; S. Brandl: 64; G. Deubzer: 16, 17, 20, 33, 37, 48, 49, 116, 116/117; Gildow: 74 bottom; Robert Harding Picture Library: 47, 59, 115; Horstmüller: 50 (bottom right); Lufthansa: 102; The Photographer's Library: 108; Pirkelmann: 32; E. Schiele: 8, 11; O. Schweisgut: 18; Scuitto: 74 top; Zela: 95.

The extracts from *Haltung des Reit und Zuchtpferdes* by Erika Schiele (BLV Verlagsgesellschaft) on the subjects of 'The sick horse' (pages 116–117) and 'Insurance' (pages 124–125) are included by kind consent of the author

Artwork: Ulrik Schramm

Published by
Octopus Books Limited
Michelin House
81 Fulham Road
London SW3 6RB

Title of the original German edition *Richtig Reiten* by Selma Brandl with Marlene Baum

English translation first published in 1989

ISBN 0 7064 5009 4

Produced by Mandarin Offset
Printed and bound in Hong Kong

Contents

Introduction

There are countless books available on the subject of learning to ride, but no-one learns to ride with book in hand, nor exclusively by actually riding. A riding manual can never replace experience but can supplement it with explanations and information. This book doesn't claim to be a comprehensive teacher, but simply attempts to introduce the uninformed reader to the horse as a creature with its own very special characteristic behaviour.

Only if you know and understand horses' needs can you really be at ease with them, learn to ride properly, and in some measure protect horses and others from accidents.

If you hope to ride well, you should know how to treat your horse properly, and you will find that intimacy with the animal and caring for it is every bit as fascinating as riding itself, for riding is only one part of horsemanship as a hobby.

By good riding we mean neither exclusively riding for fun, nor monotonous drill in the schooling area, nor hunting for laurels, but a happy, varied and as far as possible natural companionship with the horse as partner.

The best riding teachers, better than any book and many an instructor, are of course horses themselves, provided you are prepared to accept them as teachers, observe them and understand them.

Riding requires sensitivity, and sensitivity will only come with care and patience. You must accept that riding is a lifelong apprenticeship.

Good riding implies recognising horses' natures and using skill and comprehension to make them do as you, the rider, want. Good riding also means accepting responsibility for an animal that is neither a toy, nor a pet, nor a fashion accessory, and certainly not a piece of sports or professional equipment. Only if horses are correctly managed and ridden do they permit us to share their true nature and be partners in our sport and pastime, helping us daily to achieve increasing success and pleasure.

Horses' natures

You can't ride well and treat a horse properly unless you understand its nature and how this affects its behaviour.

Even stabled horses have preserved many behaviour patterns of the herd animals they originally were. Horses feel happiest when they are among their own kind, that is, when they can hear, see, smell and if possible also touch them. People must therefore put themselves in the horse's place and not try to judge them according to the standards of human logic and requirements.

Horses are grazing, herding, plains-dwelling animals, whose defence strategy is flight. The characteristics that enable them to herd and flee successfully explain not only nearly all their behaviour patterns and needs, but also their physical build.

All free-roaming horses establish a hierarchy by disputes among themselves. The dominant animal can be recognised by its particular alertness

Points of the horse

1 withers
2 shoulder
3 neck
4 breast
5 elbow
6 forearm
7 knee
8 cannon bone
9 fetlock
10 hoof
11 loins
12 croup
13 flank
14 stifle joint
15 gaskin: inner thigh musculature, visible only from behind
16 hock

The horse is a creature of flight

Flight demands speed, and speed demands long legs and a slender, streamlined body, characteristics that humans describe as 'thoroughbred' and 'noble', and admire in others besides horses! But it is not only physical build that is vital to speed, but also care of internal organs with clean air and well regulated temperature. The horse's nostrils are surrounded with very delicate skin, and are therefore extremely elastic.

To prevent overheating when running long and fast, the horse, like humans, can sweat through its skin; the sweat then evaporates and provides a cooling effect.

Haflinger ponies need their outings, particularly in winter

Biting and kicking

Horses do this only to establish their relative strengths in hierarchy disputes, or as a last defence if it is too late for flight. Even in the confines of the riding school, rank rivals threaten each other with appropriate facial expressions when they meet.

Horses are peaceable by nature and resort to biting and kicking only when wrongly treated. (See p.123.)

Fighting can often be just playfulness

The horse is a plains-dweller

Plains are partly covered with tall grass and horses have high-set necks to provide as good a range of vision as possible. Their eyes command a much wider angle than humans', for example, since they are set at the sides of their heads.

Their ears can move in all directions independently of each other, so that they can always orientate themselves on all sides.

Horses have hard hooves, the horny outer layer of which wears down naturally on the plains. In tamed horses blacksmiths regulate this

A stallion exhibits his typically impressive behaviour

natural wear (see p.28, hoof care).

Horses' long tails and manes are not simply decorative, but help to ward off insects. Their skin is highly sensitive, and by localised twitching horses can shake off parasites.

In addition to extremely sharp hearing, horses have a very keen sense of smell, and also long whiskers round their muzzle and eyes, although the significance of these hasn't been sufficiently researched yet. These fine senses provide instant warning of possible danger.

The horse's face as nature intended. Note the 'moustache'

The horse is a herd animal

The herd offers safety; animals in one can help each other. For example, foals and weak members can be kept in the middle and so protected from danger. The members of the herd can warn each other of danger and keep watch; the animals never all lie down at the same time, not even in a stable – there is always at least one on the alert.

To live successfully in a community horses must accept subordination, and nature has endowed them with the inclination to do so. A clear hierarchy reigns within the herd, each animal having its determined place. If a new horse breaks into the herd it will not be gladly welcomed immediately, but must first establish its rank.

Often two or three horses will form a regular friendship, grazing in close proximity, caressing each other's coats, and calling when they are separated. Understanding within the herd is communicated by visible and audible signals such as facial expressions or movements and various sounds. These signals are not only there for peaceful communication, such as a mutual invitation to scratch, greeting each other, playing, settling rank disputes and so on, but can also be mutual warnings between potential foes.

A resting herd of ponies makes a harmonious scene

Visible communication

Posing

The warning pose, with lifted head, erect ears, tense muscles and raised tail, indicates danger. All horses react accordingly and are immediately poised for flight. If one begins to run, all the rest follow. The dreaded bolting of horses is flight and has a contagious effect.

Facial expressions

Ear play betrays a lot about a horse. Pricked ears mean alertness, ears turned backwards can show concentration on the rider, but may also indicate pain. Ears drooping sideways show that a horse is apathetic, maybe because it is drowsy or sick. Floppy ears are a characteristic of certain breeds.

The threat expression is made with laid-back ears, raised corners of the mouth and bared teeth. Such a threatening horse should only be touched by someone who knows it! A horse's eyes say a lot about its state of mind, readily expressing contentment or anxiety.

Ear-play

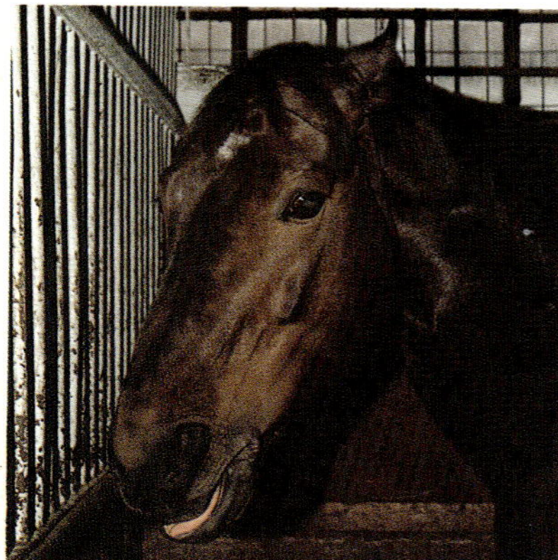

Threat

A pony's roguish little eye

Audible communications

Neighing

This is exclusively a greeting or call signal. Horses don't neigh for fear or when danger threatens, as so often inaccurately shown in cowboy films, particularly.

Snorting

Fear makes horses snort, the air puffing and whistling out of their nostrils. They also test unfamiliar objects or smells in this way. Snorting has several meanings, varying expression to show contentment or relief. When it is more like a humming it expresses tenderness, as between mare and foals.

Squealing

This is heard at times for greetings or during play; many horses also squeal when rearing or jumping.

Horses' needs

Horses are creatures of habit; they have many behaviour patterns that they manifest regularly when roaming free and which obviously make them feel good. One of these is the so-called social grooming, in which two horses stand head to tail, each zealously nibbling the places the other can't reach. In the same posture they flick flies off each other.

Rolling is a cleaning action – although many pony and horse owners might find it hard to believe! Horses in fact love a good roll in the mud, because it first scours the coat, then sticks to and removes dead hairs and skin particles. Stabled horses should therefore be given the opportunity to roll as often as possible.

Tame horses have kept many of the herd animal's behaviour patterns, but in the stable they are deprived of practically all of them.

Stabled horses often lack light as most stables are much too dark; air (horses don't feel as well as most humans do in a warm, smelly atmosphere; in fact it even makes them ill); exercise, getting only an hour's work a day, one day off a week, and inactivity for the rest of the time; physical contact with other horses, being kept caged away from their own kind; the opportunity to eat continuously, to which their digestive system is geared and last but not least the constantly changing stimuli provided by nature. Horses are, in fact, curious. They really enjoy different experiences, provided they aren't required to renounce their habits. Habit is supremely important to them; feeding, working and sleeping times ought to be regular.

Horses have good long memories, but can't reason. Riders who wait until they dismount before punishing their horse for any misdeed make a grave mistake. It is only effective to praise or scold immediately. Well trained horses will recognise a stern tone of voice as punishment, or a titbit, dismounting or patting as praise.

Horses have a fine sense of smell and find perfume or tobacco fumes

A horse dozing on its feet

equally repellent. They are also quite capable of catching the scent of fear on a person!

Horses need tenderness, but they should never be spoilt. It is wrong to believe, for example, that rain or cold harm them. Horses often prefer to stand out in the rain rather than go into the stable. In the wild they tend to seek out particularly windy places to sleep. Horses don't like hard ground. Grasslands are springy, whereas street paving is crippling – but a street is always better than sharp gravel.

Mare with sleeping foal

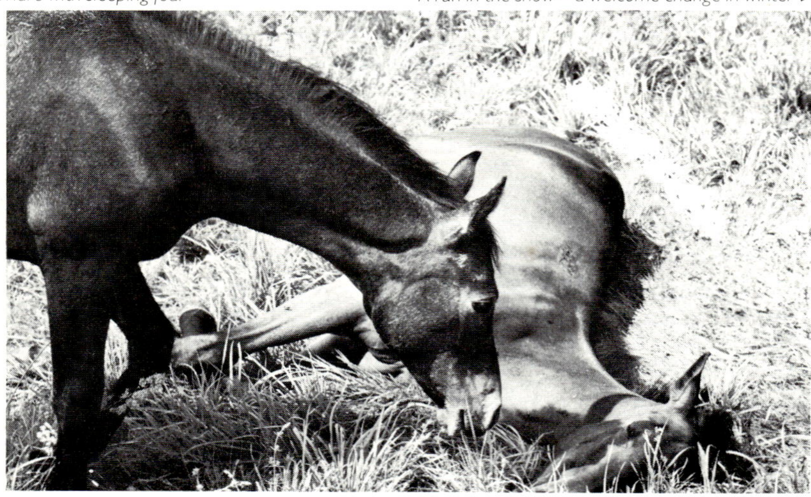

A run in the snow – a welcome change in winter ▷

Exercise

After providing water, fodder and shelter, you are responsible for providing your horse with adequate exercise.

It needs exercise to keep its organs, muscles, limbs and circulation in good health. If people don't adequately exercise their horses they are putting not only their animals' health but also their mental well-being at risk. A great deal of misbehaviour and stubbornness in fact stems from horses' reaction to lack of exercise and consequent boredom.

Adequate exercise means primarily regular, daily, varied exercise. Even on its so-called day off it is best to let a horse run round freely in the schooling area or paddock.

Adequate exercise also means that horses must be exercised carefully and under supervision. In particular, avoid excessive and frequent jumping, go at walking pace on hard ground and stop every so often for a rest.

It is also important that at least once a week a horse is given the chance to let off steam without a rider, if possible in the open air, and have a good roll about.

It depends largely on how it is exercised whether a horse is worn out by the time it is eight years old, or whether you can still get some fun out of it when it is twenty.

Lastly, horses are fundamentally herd animals and therefore gregarious – they only feel happy within sight and sound of their own kind. It is cruel to keep a horse, for example, alone in a garage behind a house. Let it have company – friendships have been known between horses and hares, horses and goats, and horses and donkeys.

Come on, stand up! We want to go for a ride!

Handling horses

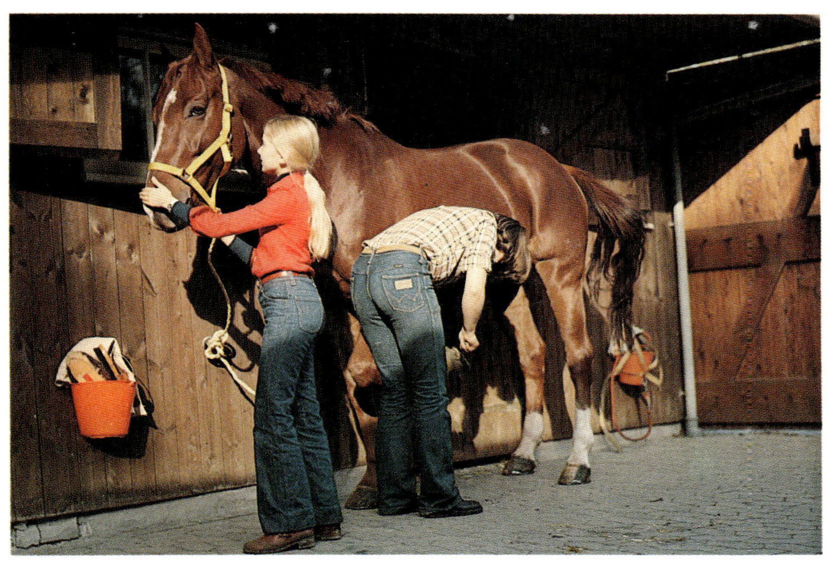

The horse's behaviour patterns and characteristics indicate how best to approach it. Establishing the right manner towards horses is the basis of learning to ride. You need to be familiar with how horses look and behave out in the fields, in the stable, at rest, taking exercise and relating to people, and why they behave as they do and not otherwise.

Above all you must constantly bear in mind that the horse is a creature of flight and is very easily startled; only then can you protect other people, yourself and the horse from accidents.

Trust

The first important thing is to win a horse's trust and affection. One way to do this is by giving it a lot of attention. The human voice also plays an important part. Of course the horse can't understand language, but is sensitive enough to know from the tone of voice whether it is being praised or rebuked, and whether the rider is inwardly worked up or is calm and unhurried.

Irritation, haste, fear, and loud shouting only upset horses, and so do sudden movements and wild gestures. Horses really enjoy soft speaking, singing, calm movements and physical contact.

Approach the horse carefully but positively

The correct way to hold a rope lead

Approaching a horse correctly

You should never approach a horse from behind without speaking to it gently, otherwise it may take fright and react instinctively. When you approach a horse speak to it and offer it the palm of your hand to smell. You can put a titbit on your open palm to prevent your fingertips being nibbled by mistake!

If the horse threatens, it is best to keep at a safe distance, especially if you haven't met it before.

Leading

To lead a horse you need a bridle and a rope that you hold in both hands, for even the calmest horse can take fright, and then it becomes impossible to grab the bridle.

As a rule you should lead a horse from its left, walking close to its shoulder, which is the safest place from which to lead.

If the horse is bridled, lead it by taking both reins in your left hand and using your right index and third finger to keep the reins apart below the snaffle ring.

When leading a horse you shouldn't look at it.

There is no reason why even a super-fit horse should not be allowed to graze a little
Note how unobtrusively the groom is handling the horse

Going out to grass

It is best not to let a horse loose until it is right in the fields, not just in the stable yard.

You should always fetch two horses together from pasture. Remember the herd instinct: one horse alone is reluctant to leave the others.

Tying up

For tying up you must always use a halter and rope, even when the horse is shut up. If horses are alarmed they want to run away and will tear themselves free so they should never be tied to movable or badly fixed objects such as door handles, box doors or loose fence posts, not even momentarily. Horses have even been known to pull large gates after them! For this reason a horse should never under any circumstances be tied by the snaffle, even though all the cowboys in Western films do so. The horse could do itself a terrible injury.

It is best, if possible, not to leave a tied horse standing alone, but to keep an eye on it.

For securing the rope you use a safety shackle and a quick-release knot, so that the horse can be freed quickly if necessary.

It is also sensible to use a leather head-collar rather than one made of colourful, unbreakable artificial material, for in an emergency it's preferable to have a broken halter than a wounded horse.

Horses shouldn't wear a halter when out to grass, because they could easily get caught up with it.

Tethers are best attached with a safety shackle

Secure quick-release knot

Lifting a hoof

For this you must position yourself facing the horse's tail, close to the leg concerned, and run a hand from the shoulder or croup, as the case may be, stroking first outwards, then inwards and downwards to the fetlock, saying, 'foot'. Most horses will recognise this and lift the required leg of their own accord. If not, gently pat the limb and lift the hoof backwards and upwards. If the hoof has to stay up for a long time you should support the horse's limb on your thigh. When lifting a hind hoof the leg should be simultaneously pulled backwards. This stops the horse kicking, because for that it needs to swing the leg first.

Normally hooves are not picked out while there is a rider in the saddle. It is remarkable how trusting and relaxed this horse is, despite the tournament atmosphere

Error

- Lifting the hind legs too high. The rider should kneel down.

The correct position for picking out a hoof

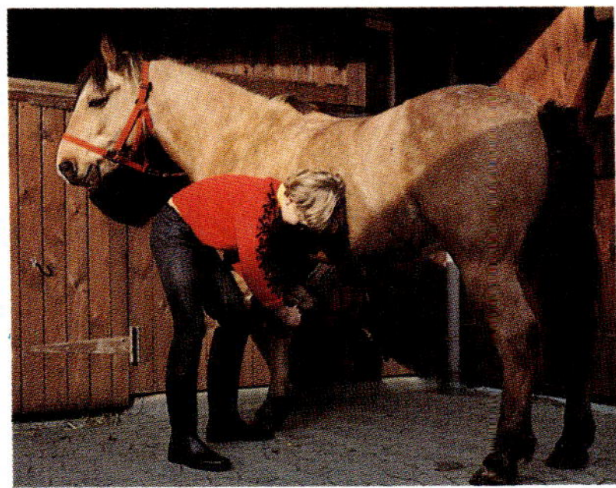

Grooming

Riding is only one element of horsemanship.

> Grooming is every bit as important as riding, doing good to horse and rider alike.

The horse should be thoroughly massaged. This will not only make you nice and warm, but if grooming is done correctly it is practically a form of fitness training, quite apart from the fact that in this way you enjoy close contact with your horse. Working so

The horse clearly shows by its expression that it is enjoying this treatment

closely on your horse also provides you with the chance to notice small wounds or skin trouble. In addition, not only do horses feel all the better for a clean-up, but it is very satisfying to see them well groomed. Lastly, it is of course pleasanter to ride a nice clean horse.

Grooming a grass-kept horse

Horses that stay out in the field should be groomed less, as the fatty layer of the skin is essential to them as weather protection. They should only be brushed and, when casting their coat, curried to remove the loose hair. Leg hair, tail and mane should never be clipped, because they provide protection against damp, cold and flies. To make the coat shiny, before an outing for instance, it may be rubbed with a few drops of sunflower oil on a woollen cloth.

Grooming a stabled horse

It is advisable to groom a stabled horse daily, for its coat can't be cleaned by the elements, and there is no opportunity for the horse to roll, scratch against bushes or indulge in mutual grooming.

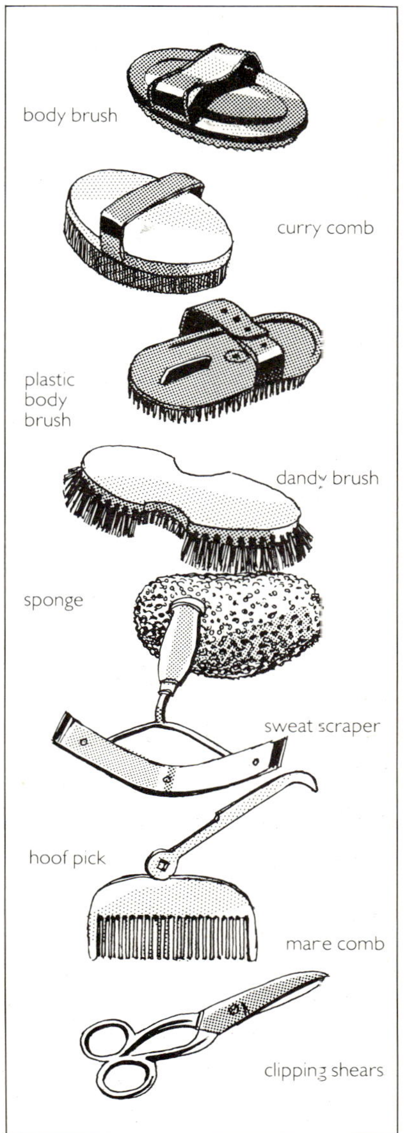

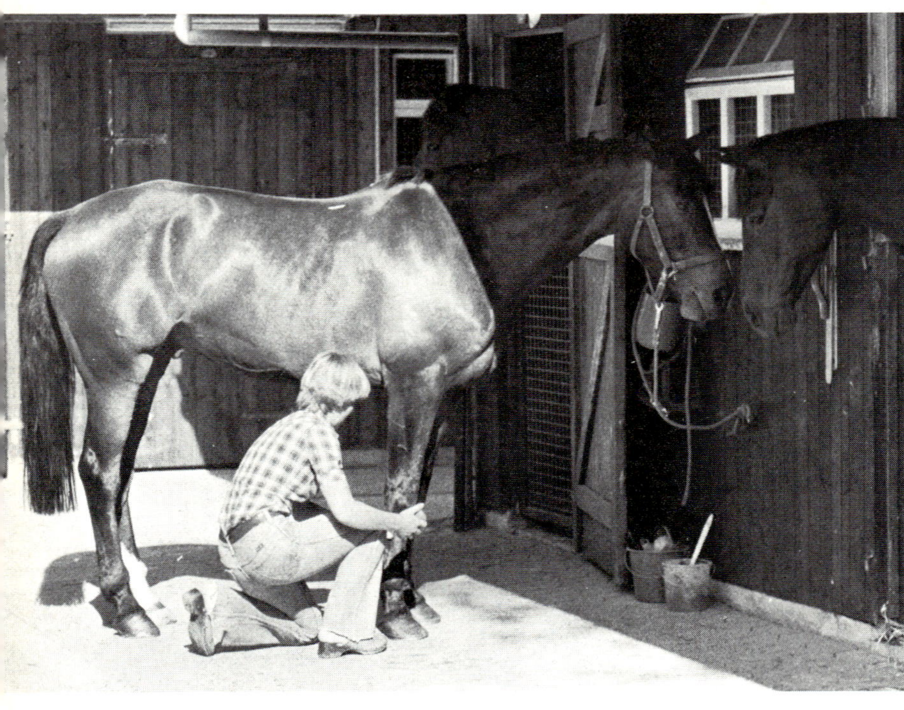

Horses should stand still and quietly during grooming. This happens when they are tended professionally. This groom is even kneeling down, which shows she is very sure of her horse's behaviour

So humans must take over the job of cleaning and massage, before riding and especially afterwards if the horse has sweated. It is also very important to look after the saddle and harness carefully, so that no dirt or sweat can cause chafing.

Skin care

When grooming a horse take it into the open air if possible, so that the dust can blow away.

As a rule, grooming begins with picking out the hooves in the loose box to prevent the stable corridor being dirtied when the horse is led out. Using a blunt hoof-pick, carefully remove any remains of droppings from the hooves, ensuring that the tool doesn't damage the frog or the frog groove. (There is more about hoof care on p.28.)

Now you can take the horse outside. First it must be brushed, using the metal body-brush with a vigorous circular motion over neck and rump, which the horse usually finds pleasant. Legs and other bony parts such as withers and haunches should never be worked with the metal brush.

Nor should it be used on ticklish horses or else they will be irritated and pointlessly distressed.

Every so often bang the brush on the floor (not the walls) to knock out the dirt.

Next brush the whole body with the dandy-brush to make the coat shine. Only the head, which is often tender, shouldn't be groomed with this hard whalebone or wooden brush. Then cleanse the horse carefully with the curry comb and the woollen cloth.

Now begins the real cleaning. Brush the whole horse down with the soft brush, working with the lie of the coat and removing hairs and skin particles after every stroke by cleaning the brush on the curry comb, which you hold in your other hand. It is best to see this brushing demonstrated before trying it yourself. It takes quite a long time, depending on how dirty the horse is, but the animal should find it very pleasant if it is affectionately done.

The special sponge is used to wash out eyes, nostrils and anus.

It is particularly important to wash the anus of horses which chafe their tails, because they do that when they have worms or are poorly groomed.

Mane and tail

You must brush these only with the curry-comb, as a comb or dandy brush would pull out far too many hairs. When brushing the tail, you should gather all the hairs and hold them firmly in your left hand and brush the ends first, as they are usually matted, then work gradually higher. If you brush the tail straight from the top too many hairs will be dragged out. In warm weather the long hair may be occasionally washed with a nourishing shampoo, but otherwise it just needs brushing.

Stabled horses can have their manes and tails dressed, the mane being pulled, where the long hair is disentangled with the help of the mane comb. Manes should never be cut, which would inevitably produce 'steps' and look unnatural.

You can pull tail hairs projecting sideways as for the mane or clip them level using curved shears so that the horse can't be wounded. You should grease the tail dock afterwards to stop the stubble tickling.

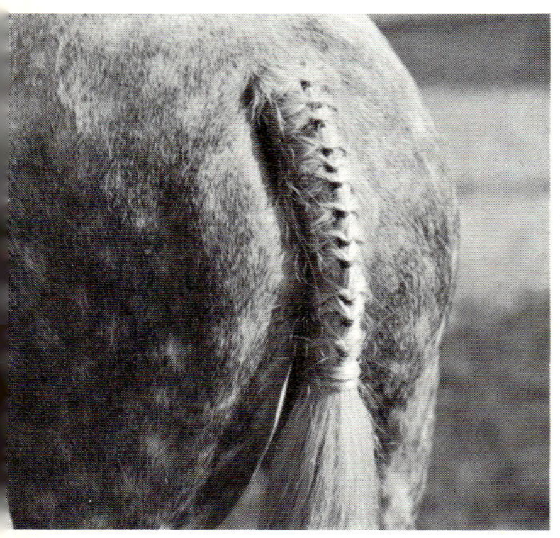

This kind of tail plaiting certainly takes some practice, but no-one should shirk the effort of trimming a horse well for a tournament

You can also trim the tail to a desired length. To do this give the tail a good brushing, then grasp all the hairs together at the dock and run your hand downwards. Then cut the hair-tips off diagonally upwards and towards the horse at about the height of the fetlock joint. The hairs will hang level when the horse lifts its tail as it moves.

If you have plenty of time you can 'select' the tail, by taking it in your left hand and carefully separating out each individual hair with your right. It does, of course, take a long time, but afterwards the tail looks very thick and silky.

Mane dressing isn't required for grass-kept horses, ponies and Arabs.

Hoof care

This is particularly important for a horse's well-being and performance.

Every four to eight weeks hooves must be trimmed and if necessary hammered by a blacksmith to prevent the growing horn being worn irregularly or getting too long. You should keep an eye on the horn in case it is growing unevenly.

You need to pick out the hooves frequently, as the frog is easily rotted by damp droppings. This can be recognised by the evil smelling wrinkles and cracks and the frogs becoming very deep. Prevent frog-rot by disinfecting the hoof-soles from time to time.

Stabled horses should have their hooves washed daily if possible, and oiled occasionally with bay rum. Oiling is especially necessary round the coronet and under the sole, it being from here that the horn grows.

Riders can sometimes be found working on their horse's hooves with a wire brush. This is not an article that belongs in the cleaning basket – these people would not treat their own fingernails in such a way!

In bad weather the hooves of grass-kept horses can also be treated with resin and grease. In any case it is important to check them regularly for foreign bodies.

Washing

Lazy keepers wash their horses instead of grooming them – but in summer a stabled horse may be sprayed every now and again provided it consents. Many horses enjoy showering down after work, while others are obviously water-shy, so you should limit yourself – and the water pressure – accordingly.

Washing with shampoo is inadvisable, because it disturbs the natural skin function.

After washing, wipe the water off with the sweat scraper, but take care over bony parts. Finally it is essential to walk the horse until it is dry.

This horse is finding a cool shower pleasant

Instead of washing, what about a ride in the warm summer rain? Firstly, riding in the rain is a pleasure, and secondly rain is more natural than a cold water spray and a washing agent.

Alternatively, if horses have been ridden hard and sweated, you can sponge them down with a damp sponge. This is particularly necessary in the saddle and girth area, all over the head, behind the ears, and between the hind legs. Here again walk the horse until the coat is dry. It is useless trying to dry a wet horse with straw, because it doesn't absorb the damp quickly.

Showering down the legs is to be recommended in any case, as it massages and cools the sinews. It is essential to dry the fetlock joint afterwards to prevent scurf forming.

Finish the cleaning process by giving the whole horse a polish with a woollen cloth, which removes any remaining dust and imparts a lovely sheen.

In conclusion, a word about using a vacuum cleaner. This speeds things up of course, but it is unnatural and impersonal. Anyone who keeps a horse shouldn't deny themselves the pleasure of grooming it in a natural way. It is also good exercise for both rider and horse.

Rolling is an expression of well-being

Stabling and feeding

Stabling

Most stables are planned rather from the point of view of human beings than orientated towards the needs of the horse.

Given that stabling is a necessary evil for domesticated horses, it should, as far as possible, take into account what we know of horses' natures and preferences.

The ideal stable is high, light, airy, dry and cool, and allows the horse at least a little room to move about.

Horses should be housed in roomy loose boxes or long stables with windows that the animals can look out of. This prevents boredom and infections of the respiratory tract.

Above all, horses must be able to see each other from their stalls, which means that loose boxes with high, closed sides that prevent any contact with neighbours are wrong for them.

Tethering to a post is to be avoided – it is not only dangerous, but conflicts with all natural behaviour.

A long stable, on the other hand, takes account of the horses' natural need for contact with their fellows, but isn't suitable for race horses, there being too much disturbance and risk of injury.

Good long stables of this type are unfortunately rare. Every horse owner should, however, consider whether there is any possibility of creating more natural stable conditions – for the good of the horse.

Leisure horses, which get less exercise and are alone for much of the time, are best housed together in a stable building, though it is necessary to find out beforehand how the individual animals get on with each other, and think what it involves in social behaviour, to accommodate a number of horses together permanently. Long stables undoubtedly make more work, but they are better for the horse.

Bedding

Another thing that is best for the horse although labour intensive is the customary straw bedding. Droppings and wet straw must be removed and fresh straw strewn on top. Eventually an absorbent mattress is built up, the bottom layer consisting of damp dung while the top layer is fresh and clean. Not only does this litter have the advantage of being warm and dry, but the horses always have something to nibble, too.

Obviously the straw needs attention several times a day. Foul-smelling, rotten straw has no place in the stable, only on the dungheap. Finally, remember that only we humans enjoy a warm stable odour; it makes horses ill.

If, however, horses have to stand on peat or sawdust they must always be given raw fodder – hang up a hay-net. You might even consider man-made flooring, which is the easiest to maintain and no worse for the horse than peat or sawdust.

Outdoor management

Some hardy breeds can live out of doors the whole year round, provided they have a shelter to protect them from wind, wet, and insects.

The entrance must be shielded from wind and the interior dry.

Feeding and watering

Watering

Nearly all stables now have automatic drinking troughs. This spares you having to lug water-buckets about and enables the horse to drink as often and as much as it likes, but doesn't altogether solve the water problem. The water troughs must, in fact, be checked and cleaned daily or else they smell stale and attract bacteria. Horses are very demanding about their drink, and need clean, fresh water for their well-being.

Watering from a bucket is time and energy consuming, but it does enable you to check how much the horse is drinking, and furthermore the water is cleaner than in an unsupervised automatic trough.

Sick horses should always be watered from a bucket to prevent the passing on of infection from an automatic trough.

The ideal is a well in the stable, to which the horse is led to drink, which also provides an additional reason for the horse to leave its loose box now and again.

Feeding

Free-roaming horses constantly eat small quantities of easily digested food. They have small stomachs and sensitive intestines.

In the stable they are given concentrate feed in the form of oats or a mixture of oats and mixed feed, which provide energy. The volume of food is made up with hay which provides bulk. Of course you should provide only the very best hay. It should be well tossed and offered slightly moistened. This way it makes less dust, and most horses prefer moist food. Finally, grass has high water-retention properties.

Feeding with horse cubes ('neat' or with added bran) is rather controversial. Because of their mineral content they can be used as supplementary food, but not in place of hay, since they have too low a bulk. The horse certainly gets sufficient calories, but misses a constant full-feeling in its stomach. The cubes should if possible be large ones 'briquettes' are the most digest ble.

Food quantity depends on each horse's individual needs.

Tip

- Horses should be fed as often as possible, at least three feeds a day at regular times. This is of great importance for the sound functioning of the alimentary tract. Feeding time should be peaceful and relaxed and after feeding horses should be allowed at least an hour's digestion time before being ridden.

Important

- Don't give too much high-energy food if a horse can't be exercised. It runs the risk of laminitis or azotouria. Horses who have to stand for a long time are happier if they get more hay, because it gives them something to do.

Grass-kept horses should get supplementary food in the form of energy food or hay when their pasture is inadequate or if they have to work regularly.

Salt licks

These are good for both stabled and grass-kept horses, as they top up the body's mineral reserves.

Supplementary feeds

Titbits in the form of bread, fruit, carrots, the occasional egg and some vitamin cubes (rather than sugar) are a welcome change and supplement. But don't use horses as waste disposal units; mouldy food will make them sick. Don't feed lawn mowings. You can occasionally give birch, beech,

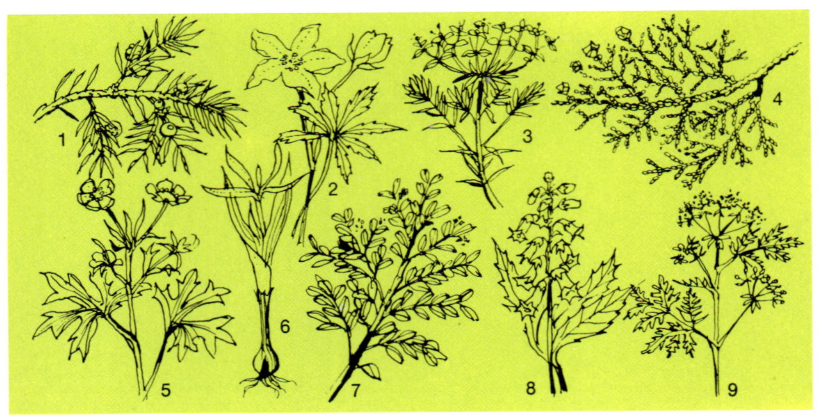

Poisonous plants:
1 yew
2 hellebore
3 spurge
4 tree of life
5 buttercup
6 autumn crocus
7 box
8 foxglove
9 hemlock

rowan, oak, spruce, horsechestnut or fir twigs to nibble, as they contain essential oils, bitter principle and tannin.

Mash

Once a week a horse should get a warm meal – this is in fact a very English habit.

Recipe

Soak a large cupful of linseed in plenty of water for 24 hours, then bring it to the boil. (Take care, it catches easily.) As soon as the first bubble appears, add some cold water and bring back to the boil. Lastly stir it into a thick mash with some bran, oats and if necessary more warm water. Serve warm.

Refusing food

Horses will indicate all sorts of problems by refusing their food. It could be mental disturbance, physical exhaustion, feverish illness or tooth trouble. If even mash, bran sops, titbits, carrots or apples are not accepted it is time to call the vet.

If there is no grass, try some sprays of fir for a change

Finding a riding stable

Enquiring for a good riding stable is of prime importance when learning to ride. If you go by certain points it is possible to get quite an accurate idea even without any specialist knowledge. You can confidently let yourself be led by your feel of the atmosphere.

- A good stable is light, tidy and clean.
- The horses are well fed and calm, look contented, and live in well littered loose boxes.
- There is a schooling area at least 20 × 40 metres, an open yard, and territory to ride out in.
- Equestrian activities are taught.
- The school horses work a maximum of three hours a day, four on exceptional occasions.
- Classes ('rides') comprise no more than eight riders.

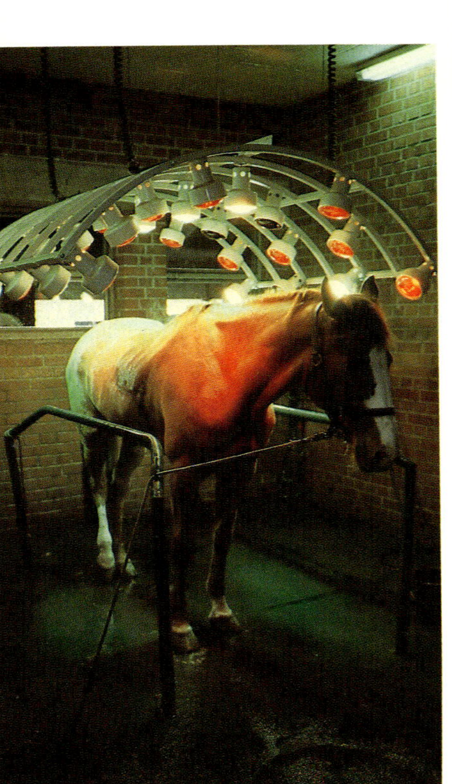

A few stables nowadays are equipped with a solarium. They make horses feel well and relaxed, and a session before riding could help to solve many problems

The most important part of a good riding stable is not the clubroom but the atmosphere. It stands or falls by a good instructor and good school horses. To ride a school horse that you know is being ridden six hours a day is deliberate cruelty to animals. A riding-stable owner who lends horses to any and every customer is guilty of such cruelty. Unfortunately this really needs stressing. Riding means accepting the responsibility for a creature that is your partner in the sport or pastime you have chosen. Learning to ride takes a long time and costs patience, effort, courage and discipline. In the long run it is better to take time to find the right stable than settle for any old convenient horse-hirer.

The riding instructor

Good riding instructors must have taken a relevant examination and have a grasp of teaching methods and some understanding of psychology.

They should be able to express themselves clearly and understandably – without ever feeling the need to shout.

There are various types and level of riding instructors depending on what sort of training the riding concern offers and to what sort of learner.

- Assistant instructors – BHSAI
- Intermediate instructors – BHSII
- Fellow of the British Horse Society – FBHS

There are, however, many uncualified instructors who have a wealth of experience and knowledge to impart.

Riding instructors need a great deal of patience and persistence, and must always be ready to explain, and above all to ensure that their pupils concern themselves with the horses outside the riding lesson, for, as we have seen, associating with them is every bit as important as the riding itself.

A good instructor should
- divide rides into grades.
- teach using a variety of methods and exercises.
- take beginners on the lunge or long rein (see p.61) for the first few hours.
- check saddles and reins before the lesson.
- be neither irascible nor unfair in treatment of the horses.
- allow pupils eventually to take part in small tournaments.

A good instructor will inspire pupils to enjoy riding and, despite disappointments, always to look forward to the next lesson, and set an example to them both as a rider and in a wider context.

Most children approach horses with fearless confidence, and horses for their part seem concerned and careful

The school horse

Without question the best teacher is always the old, well trained mount, whose good character, health and sound basic training are more important than its beauty. It should move smoothly and be good tempered, not too lazy, sure-footed, manageable and quiet.

School horses are hard workers with a patient temperament. They are used to trouble with their beginners and need particular love and care.

Horses motivate each other when quadrille riding. Often old school horses that have grown listless bloom again when exercised to music in a group

The rider

'Chivalrous' comes from 'chevalier' or 'cavalier', literally meaning 'horseman'. All riders should cultivate the chivaleresque virtues of courtesy, modesty and courage.

Riding involves a relationship with another creature, which shouldn't be blamed when things go wrong. Mistakes are nearly always a rider's, not a horse's, fault.

There is no need to advertise that you ride by clanking your spurs along the street. Spurs should only be worn while on horseback, and then only if absolutely necessary.

It is all too easy to antagonise people on foot by arrogantly and thoughtlessly galloping through mud and puddles. Good riders are always considerate towards horse, riding companions and other people on foot.

Good horsemanship is not fostered by drinking alcohol or abusing and blaming your horse or riding instructor when things don't go well.

A rider's best virtues are patience and modesty; a good rider should delight in even the smallest pleasure and progress; be helpful, and be more concerned about a horse than an audience.

Beginners in the schooling area

Joining a ride

This provides a good transition from training on the lunge to riding alone.

Once you are secure enough on the lunge and have learnt to influence your horse actively, your instructor will take you into a beginner's ride. The easiest way for you to try out and to some extent independently make use of what you have learnt is by riding behind a practised beginner, for in the ride the horses follow the herd instinct and the riding-instructor's voice and proceed calmly and steadily one behind another. This provides you with ample opportunity to let yourself be carried along and concentrate on your seat. In the ride beginners learn to steer and govern their horses, observe the safety distance from the rider ahead and ensure that their horse carries out the various school figures correctly.

Solo riding

When you have gained a little confidence in this group (without your seat having suffered), the instructor will let you perform individual exercises. At this point you will need to learn some precise signals, known as aids, to direct and control your horse independently of the instructor. You need to be able to ride alone confidently before venturing beyond the riding school.

Structure of a riding lesson

An hour's lesson is generally divided into three 20-minute phases:

- Warm-up and preparation
- Main section
- Winding down and relaxing.

Warm-up

Loosening and limbering exercises for both rider and horse: walking on a long rein, gentle trotting, riding wide turns, changing pace.

Remember to tighten the girth!

Main section

Learning new lessons, exercises to improve and perfect the aids. Include a short rest before the main phase is over, before the end of an exercise that horse and rider have performed well, for every lesson should close with a successful experience for both.

Winding down

Give the horse its head, praise it, ride at a walk, if possible in countryside ride or lead it at ambling pace. After dismounting loosen the girth, raise the stirrups and make the horse comfortable.

The schooling area

This is a rectangular arena 20 metres (70 feet) wide and 40 or 60 metres (140 or 210 feet) long. It can be open-air or indoor. The perimeter is known as the fence. Inside the fence runs the outer track, usually well trodden and recognisable. Alongside, about 1 ½ metres (5 feet) away, lies the inner track.

- Inside means the side facing the centre of the arena.
- Outside means the side facing the fence.
- Riding on the right hand means riding round to the right.
- Riding on the left hand means riding round to the left.
- The arena is divided and labelled with various spots and letters, which also represent marker points for the school figures.

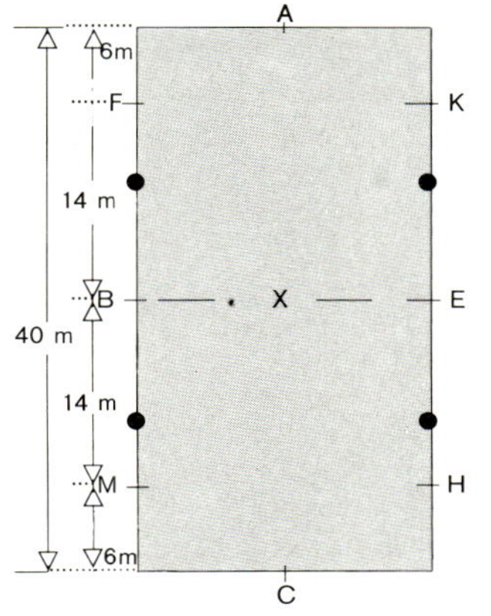

Rules

Behaviour in the schooling area is governed by certain rules that are important for the safety of both riders and horses:

- Riders entering or leaving the arena must knock or ask if the doorway is free and wait for an answer.
- Mounting and dismounting must be done in the middle of the circle.
- When walking, the outer track must always be left free unless riders are using it.
- The rider on the left has precedence.
- When a number of riders are using the arena it is better if all ride round the same way. In this case the instructor or the senior rider will call for a change of direction about every 5 minutes.
- Safety and politeness should be paramount
  - Be careful, attentive and considerate to others
  - Be tolerant towards young horses and inexperienced riders; practised riders can control a horse better than beginners
  - Always keep a safe distance behind the animal in front
  - Always keep a safe distance sideways

• = circle points
F-K-M-H = tangents

School figures

The following school figures are recognised:

Whole arena CMBFAKEH (right hand)

Half arena CMBXEH (right hand)

Long side MF or KH (right hand)

Short side Both sides of C or both sides of A

Middle line (lengthways) CXA or AXC

Diagonal line across entire arena MXK or FXH

Diagonal line across half arena ME or FE or KB or HB

Centre point of arena X

Circle This has a diameter of 20 metres (70 feet). The points on the circumference that the rider must pass through over a full horselength when riding on the right hand, lie at C, then halfway between the corner after C and B (10 metres/35 feet), then X, then halfway between E and the corner after H (10 metres/35 feet).

The second circle lies correspondingly between A and X.

Changing circles After completing one circle the rider goes through point X and passes automatically into the second circle.

Crossing through circle From the circumference point on the long side the rider turns through a half circle of 10 metres (35 feet) diameter, passes through the centre point of the large circle and turns through another 10-metre (35-foot) half circle back to the main circumference.

Tangents are points M, F, K and H.

Single serpentine This is a line beginning at the first tangent on a long side, curving evenly away from that side to a maximum of six paces (about 5 metres/17 feet) and curving back to the following tangent on the same side.

Two-loop serpentine This is also performed along a long side, curving away twice to a maximum of three paces each time. It starts at the first tangent on a long side, passes through B or E over one horselength of track, and ends at the following tangent. Both curves must be even.

Serpentines along entire arena Here the number of loops can be chosen. For five loops, for example, the rider must pass through three points on the track as well as the two tangents, each time over one horselength.

Volte This is a circle of six paces (about 5 metres/17 feet) diameter.

Turn out of corner This is a figure ridden like half a six-pace volte, then taking about nine paces to return to the long side.

Double volte A volte performed twice in succession.

Figure eight A volte on the right (or left) hand, followed immediately by a volte on the left (or right) hand. It is always performed around X, the centre point of the arena.

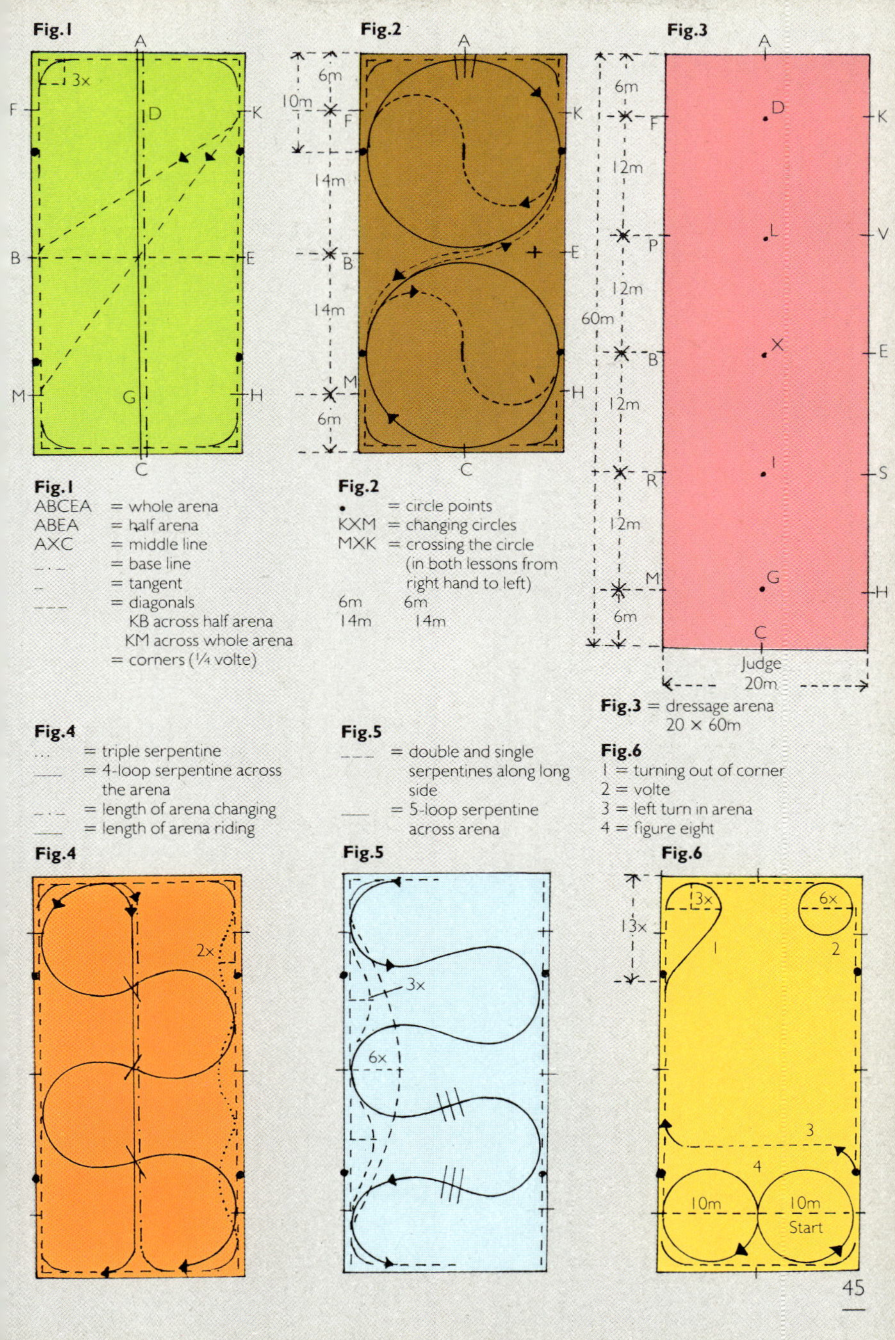

Fig.1
ABCEA = whole arena
ABEA = half arena
AXC = middle line
_ . _ = base line
_ = tangent
_ _ _ = diagonals
KB across half arena
KM across whole arena
= corners (¼ volte)

Fig.2
• = circle points
KXM = changing circles
MXK = crossing the circle (in both lessons from right hand to left)
6m 6m
14m 14m

Fig.3 = dressage arena 20 × 60m

Fig.4
... = triple serpentine
____ = 4-loop serpentine across the arena
_ . _ = length of arena changing
____ = length of arena riding

Fig.5
_ _ _ = double and single serpentines along long side
____ = 5-loop serpentine across arena

Fig.6
1 = turning out of corner
2 = volte
3 = left turn in arena
4 = figure eight

Equipment

Horse
1 Bridle with combined head collar
2 Running martingale (carefully fixed for length)
3 Breast strap
4 General-purpose saddle
5 Leather brushing boots

Rider
6 Crash helmet (essential when hacking)
7 Battle-dress style jacket
8 Riding breeches
9 Riding boots
10 Spurs
11 Gloves

Saddlery

This should on principle be practical and simple.

Old, well cared for, leather tack is better than new because it is softer and suppler. If you have to buy new, it is safer to go for known brands than cheap equipment, because safety and durability depend on the quality of the material.

For the same reasons reins and stirrup leathers should be regularly checked and the tack treated daily with saddle soap and once a week with leather oil dressing. Wet leather must dry out slowly and then be well greased.

The condition and individual suitability of saddle and bridle are very important to both horse and rider.

Correct saddling and bridling are essential for horses to feel comfortable; ill-fitting saddles or bridles can cause discomfort and even pain to horses.

Saddle

When learning to ride, a general-purpose saddle is the most suitable. It can be used equally well for dressage or for jumping. When dressage riding, this saddle gives the beginner sufficient grip and security at the knees.

A saddle must lie flat on the horse's back and be so well stuffed that it doesn't press down on the withers – otherwise it will certainly cause saddle fatigue, which is both painful and tediously persistent.

It is crucial for seat and for effect when dressage riding that the lowest point of the seat panel lies in the middle of the saddle.

Saddlery care with a difference! This is usually done in the tack room, but in fine surroundings it is more fun out of doors

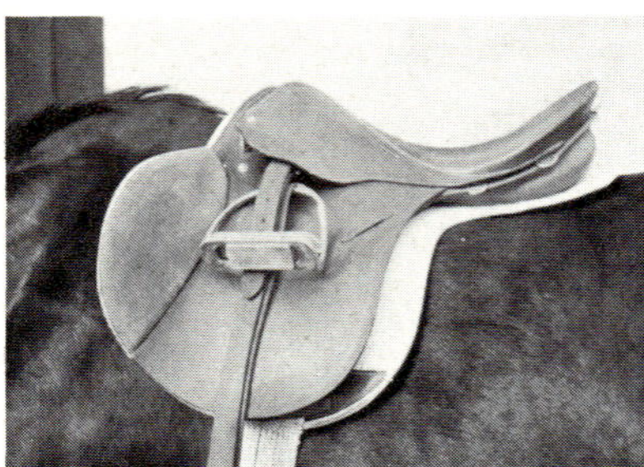

Correct position of a general purpose saddle

Saddle cloth

A saddle cloth is used beneath the saddle to soak up the sweat. It is the same shape as the saddle and fastened to it by leather loops.

Felt makes a good saddle cloth, provided the underside is regularly scraped and brushed to prevent its hardening with dirt and sweat.

Cotton or towelling, however, are very practical and hygienic, as they can easily be laundered when they are dirty and also dry more readily than felt.

Synthetic fabrics are to be avoided, as they are unpleasant to the skin and may cause allergies.

Girth

Girths are usually made of webbing, but there are also leather and elastic ones. The girth too should be regularly cleaned of all dirt and sweat that could cause sores.

Stirrups

Stirrups must be large and heavy with a rubber tread to stop the foot sliding out.

Stirrup leathers

These should be especially well looked after to make sure that they don't become brittle. The buckles they go through are left open so that the leathers can easily slip out.

The stirrup leathers should be swapped over from time to time, or else the left one, which is more strained in mounting, will wear out first.

Bridle

As a rule, the type of bridle used is a snaffle.

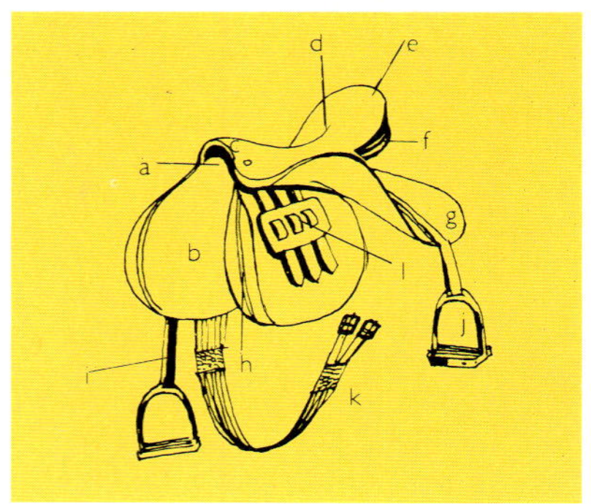

a *arch* b *panel* c *pommel*
d *seat* e *cantle* f *lining*
g *flap* h *knee roll* i *stirrup leather*
j *stirrup* k *girth* l *girth straps*

Bit

The most popular bit is the German snaffle. Its width and size must correspond to the horse's mouth. The thicker it is, the softer, and the thinner, the sharper.

A horse being bridled for the first time. The thickness and length of the snaffle should be determined beforehand by measuring the head

Noseband

This should stop the horse opening its jaws wide, thereby overcoming the effect of the reins.

Hanoverian bridle

With its dropped noseband this best fulfils this purpose, but it has the great disadvantage of hindering the horse's breathing if the noseband isn't correctly fitted.

English noseband

This lies up on the nose bone and fulfils its purpose very well on a well ridden horse feeling confident under the hand of a sensitive rider.

Mexican bridle

This is a combination of the English and Hanoverian. It has a high-sitting noseband with a curb-bit attached. It is used particularly for trekking, jumping and military horses, as it doesn't hinder breathing. Very sensitive horses often perform better with this kind of bridle.

Fitting the bridle

The bridle should be adjusted so that the mouthpiece lies exactly across the bars of the mouth without drawing up the corners of the mouth (too short) or butting against the corner incisors (too long).

In no circumstances should the headpiece make breathing difficult, neither should it prevent the horse from chewing.

As a check, two fingers should pass comfortably between the noseband and the horse's nosebone.

The throatlash should not be buckled too tight, or else it will constrict. There should be room for a fist between throat and lash.

Correctly fitting English bridle with a snaffle bit

Correctly fitting Mexican bridle with a Pelham bit

American bridle with cheek snaffle

Hanoverian bridle with a dropped noseband

Martingales

These are helpful only for good, experienced riders, otherwise their leverage effect is far too severe and only aggravates the persistence of difficulties. The less leather about the horse, the better!

Side reins

These are the only sensible auxiliaries for beginners, for they provide the horse with a constant reference when the rider's hand is still too unsteady and unskilled. If the school horse is wearing a side rein riders are less inclined to think about hand control and can concentrate on their seat.

Side reins are adjusted so that the horse's nose is held almost vertically. They are hooked onto the snaffle rings underneath the reins and buckled onto the upper half of the girth. Side reins must always be fitted before mounting.

Bitless bridles and hackamores

These aren't suitable either for beginners or for part-time riders. With their sharp leverage they belong only in the hands of sensitive experts.

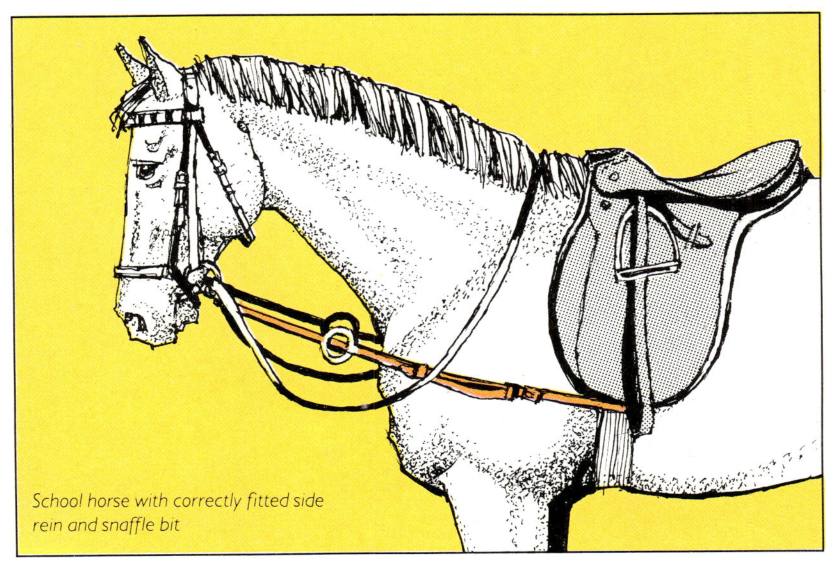

School horse with correctly fitted side rein and snaffle bit

Correct riding clothes, suitable for both sports and country

Riding clothes

These should be practical and comfortable and contribute to the aesthetic appearance of horse and rider combined. Long hair must always be tied back or coiled up.

Figure-hugging or very roomy sweaters and jackets make it more difficult to achieve a correct seat.

Suitable clothes include: plain jacket, shirt, sweater, elasticated riding breeches, rubber or leather boots, jodhpurs and ankle-boots, gloves (indispensable) and a well-fitting steel-lined riding hat. Whips and spurs (blunt ones) should only be used when strictly necessary.

(For trekking equipment see pages 108–109.)

Tacking up

Saddling

This is done from the horse's left. With shortened stirrups and loosened girth, lay the saddle carefully on the horse's withers and push it gently backwards. Then hoist the saddle cloth up under the pommel so that it too doesn't press down on the withers. When passing the girth beneath the horse, take care that it doesn't hit its forelegs, and for the moment pull it just tight enough to stop the saddle slipping. If you immediately tighten the girth fully the horse is likely to feel saddle pressure, which will cause enough anxiety to make it rear or even throw itself to the ground. Should this happen, take it for a few minutes' walk or trot to calm it down.

Bridling

Before inserting the bit, you must put the bridle on. Remove the head collar and lay the reins over the horse's head and neck. With your right hand hold the bridle in the middle of the headpiece and slip it from below up the horse's nose and over its head. Push your middle finger and thumb between the animal's lips, inducing it to open its mouth. The bit can now be pushed in while your right hand slips the headpiece first over the right ear, then over the left. Next arrange the headband and mane; the headband shouldn't press against the ears. Then buckle the throatlash so that you can comfortably insert a flat hand.

All manipulation must be done with care and firmness.

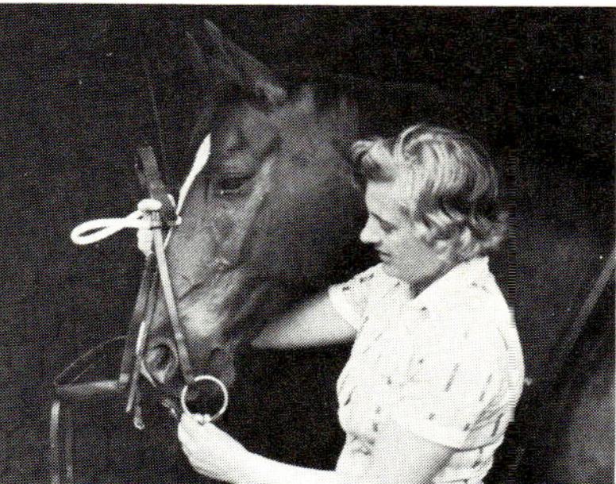

Putting on a bridle correctly

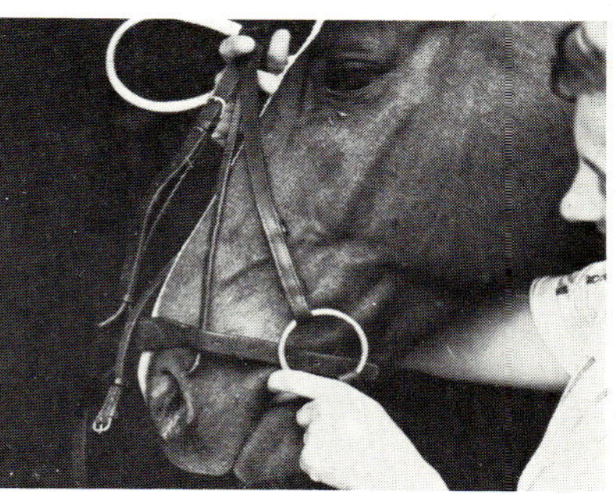

Mounting

Before you mount the horse, stand on the horse's left side with your back to the horse's head. Take the reins with your left hand and establish a light contact with the horse's mouth. This stops the horse stepping forwards. Then grasp the mane or the front of the saddle with your left hand, inserting your left foot into the stirrup after twisting it round. Grasp either the middle or edge of the saddle with your right hand. Spring off your right foot, swing your right leg over the croup and settle gently into the saddle. Then put your right foot into the right stirrup.

Sooner or later every rider needs to master mounting and dismounting even out in the country. It is part of a horse's basic training and built-up trust that it will remain steady meanwhile

Dismounting

When dismounting maintain contact with the horse's mouth; the reins lie in your left hand, which rests on the mane. Take your left foot out of the stirrup and swing your right leg over the croup, while, all in the same movement, removing your left foot from the stirrup and slipping down off the horse.

Observe the following points

- Mount calmly and slowly
- Settle gently into the saddle
- Hold the reins evenly
- Dismount without haste
- Avoid tugging the reins when descending

Learning to ride

Basics

We all know that riding means moving along on a mount. But there is a world of difference between letting ourselves be carried about by an animal and deliberately steering a horse over a course.

Riding correctly has a purely technical physical side that anyone can learn. The other element is a matter of feeling that no instructor can convey. In this chapter the physical side of riding will be explained, to make it clear what the perfect training of rider and horse aims at.

Balance and weight distribution

Without a rider a horse finds itself in a perfect balance and, just as a human being without a load or other impediment to the movement mechanism, has no difficulty in moving.

Once a rider sits on a horse both have the immediate problem of how to adjust to the new balance ratio. It isn't only the rider who has initial difficulties in balancing, but the horse too. The horse's equilibrium is influenced

- by the unfamiliar weight
- by the lack of co-ordination between its own centre of gravity and that of its rider.

Riding is fundamentally a question of balance between rider and horse.

To give a simple example: when you carry something, you try to position it exactly over your centre of gravity, because that makes carrying most easy. Anyone carrying a rucksack bends forwards; people who habitually carry heavy loads on their heads do so with remarkable elegance, walking completely upright with the load's centre of gravity directly over their own.

The problem about riding is to co-ordinate the centres of gravity of horse and rider to make it easier for the horse to carry the load and not to hinder its freedom of movement.

When the horse is standing still, the centres of gravity of horse and rider don't coincide; the rider's lies behind that of the horse. When the horse moves forwards, the faster it goes the more it extends and the further forwards its centre of gravity moves.

If a horse is badly ridden, the centres of gravity of both creatures will never coincide, so the horse will stiffen and move awkwardly and consequently the rider will sit uncomfortably, being jolted on the horse's stiff back.

78

Forward seat at the canter

There are two ways in which the horse's and rider's centres of gravity can be made to coincide. Which alternative is employed depends on what the horse is being required to perform.

- The rider shifts his or her centre of gravity over that of the horse, following the forward movement by bending the torso forwards (forward seat). This should be done when running, jumping or hacking, as the performance depends primarily on the horse, which must produce the greatest possible speed or elevation. The rider can assist its movement by entering into it and shifting their centre of gravity over that of the horse.
- The horse is induced to alter the way it holds its body, to shift its centre of gravity backwards, below that of its rider (dressage seat). This is appropriate in dressage riding, when the horse's gymnastic training comes into play. Its movement should be as beautiful and effortless as possible, and it should obey its rider in such a way that all commands are entirely unobtrusive.

The horse's gymnastic learning ultimately teaches it to walk with its hindquarters (i.e. its back legs, its 'engine') more below the centre of gravity. In this case it raises its forequarters, its step becomes statelier, more expressive, it arches its neck and drops its head until its nose is almost vertical. It looks 'rounder'. In the jargon this is called collection.

Collection will be achieved only if the horse is relaxed, never by force and restraint. Then the rider can sit relaxed and upright in the saddle, because the horse's centre of gravity coincides with their own.

Once this coincidence is achieved, both rider and horse experience a sense of effortlessness.

Once a rider has experienced the feeling of sitting on an effortlessly obedient horse, they will always be striving to repeat the experience. How often this happens will depend on the ability and training level of both horse and rider.

Every ridden horse, whether it is a holiday hire horse or a competitive mount, a pony or a jumper, should learn to be relaxed and balanced under a rider.

There are two good reasons for this:

- A horse ridden out of balance will soon suffer damage to its sinews and joints.
- Even occasional riders want to experience some communion with the horse and should be able to sit upright and relaxed in the saddle and feel a relaxed horse under them, that they can control without undue effort.

To find itself in equilibrium with its rider the horse must take a greater part of the load on its hind quarters, arch its back in a relaxed manner and let its neck drop so that its nose hangs almost vertically.

After all, a person giving a child a piggyback also curves their back upwards and drops their head to take the strain.

The horse, however, will hardly do all this on its own accord, so the rider must learn to persuade it to do so, but not through force, be it understood, for no-one can be forced to relax!

Learning phases

The three phases of learning to ride are

- Firstly establishing the correct seat on a horse, to find your own balance (see p.61).

- Learning the various means at your disposal, known as the aids, for signalling your intentions to the horse (see pp.75–80).

- Gradually learning to adjust these aids so that you finally achieve a balanced co-ordination between horse and rider (see p.79).

This fine adjustment between impulsion aids (whereby the hindquarters move further under the centre of gravity) and controlling aids (whereby the horse becomes not more hurried, but more active) demands a great deal of practice, patience, and above all sensitivity. And since each horse and each rider is different, and both may feel different on different days, learning to ride is a lifelong study!

Riding involves a co-ordination of effort between two living beings.

Apart from other aims, riding has the primary one of making their combined movement so pleasant and energy-saving to both horse and rider that they can go on to develop sporting skills or simply have fun together.

Learning to ride means learning first of all to do nothing more than sit passively. Active influence over the horse comes later, more or less automatically.

Unfortunately the correct, upright dressage seat, as described in all good riding manuals, always looks rather stiff and artificial. A beginner can be beautifully placed on a standing horse, and all the whys and wherefores can be exactly explained, but the moment the horse starts to move the picture changes. Then what really matters first is not the low heel and perfect hand position, but flexibility, a capacity for sympathetic understanding, participation in the horse's movement and a feel for balance.

Balance, relaxation and breathing exercises form a regular part of every lunging lesson

Practical riding instruction

Seat exercises

You can only learn to sense and participate in the movement of a horse if you are completely relaxed.

To give beginners the chance to achieve this, instructors will at first take them for a period on the lunge and let them just do exercises to strengthen their seat. Pupils sit on horses without reins or stirrups: they don't need reins because the handler is guiding the horse with the lunge and stirrups are also superfluous as beginners are bound to lose them. Taking to reins and stirrups too soon only hinders concentration on balance and relaxation.

Breathing and relaxing

The first stage is to practise, at the walk, breath control and relaxation to overcome anxiety and tension. For this there are all sorts of exercises that will help you to move each of your limbs independently, and at the same time give you a feeling for the mobility of individual joints: turning your head, circling your shoulders, moving arms and legs singly, circling your ankles, loosening your wrists, turning round in the saddle, standing up on the horse, lying back on the horse's quarters, or placing your arms round the horse's neck. All these exercises help you to strengthen your balance in the saddle, establish confidence with the horse and above all to locate the two supremely important seatbones on which you must sit. It is vital not to tense your seat muscles, for that automatically raises you out of the saddle. Just slip your flat hand between the saddle and your buttocks and give them a few squeezes. You will notice at once that tense muscles 'sit' less, whereas what you really have to do on the horse's back is to sit broad, deep and relaxed.

Only when you have mastered freedom at the walk, that is when your buttock muscles are relaxed, your thighs have stopped squeezing convulsively and your hips are nice and flexible, can you absorb movement at the trot, meaning that the horse will not bounce you. If, however, you are tense, hang on tight with arms and legs and hold your breath in obvious anxiety, you will be thrown up in the air at every step of the trot, because the horse too will at once make its back hard.

Once you rest in the middle of the saddle on both seatbones and let yourself be carried by the horse without tensing up, your thighs and shins will also fall into the right position, dangling loosely from your hips.

In fact, if you are sitting correctly on the horse, you won't need to hang on with your legs, and shouldn't try to do so. The truth of this has been demonstrated by the many handicapped people who sit exceptionally well on a horse despite having no strength in their legs.

Until a rider has developed enough confidence, it is permissible to hold onto the saddle when trotting or cantering

Through the various exercises on the lunge you will come to trust your own ability to move easily with the horse's gait. In the end you won't need to hang onto the saddle any more and gain confidence because you will have found equilibrium.

Tip

- Riding freehanded with your eyes closed will improve your confidence.

The correct way to fall and roll on the shoulder. The rolling movement can be braked by bracing with the forearms and at the same time lifting the legs

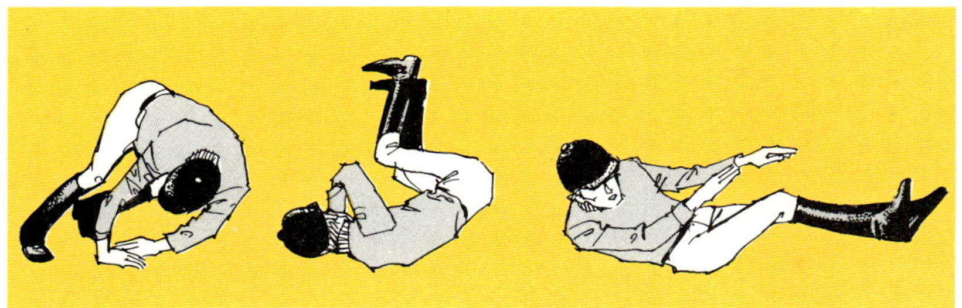

This sideways roll is a preparatory exercise and may also be practised in the schooling area

Falling and landing

Learning how to fall and land should always be included as part of riding lessons. Falls practice should be taken very seriously in the interests of preventing injury.

First practise forward rolls and backward rolls on the floor, both from a standing position and in movement, or rolls with a somersault on a mattress. Then let yourself roll off the horse or jump down.

Riders must learn to make their muscles contract and relax separately. In an emergency your body reacts automatically, provided you have trained long enough to make the right movements follow as a reflex.

Tip

- Do some relevant judo exercises!

2

Dressage seat

You can only achieve the correct seat by total relaxation, and it is crucial for the further success of your training how thorough this phase is. You will never again find it hard to hold your hands steady on the reins, even when the horse is going at a fast trot or gallop. You will also be able to carry out the instructor's seat corrections without getting tense. Now the moment has come when you gradually learn to influence the horse intentionally and actively through the aids.

An elegantly seated rider – obviously concentrating, but nevertheless relaxed

Perfecting the seat

The correct dressage seat requires you to be completely relaxed in all your muscles, and spread your weight evenly and gently over both seatbones at each of the horse's paces. The full width of your buttocks should rest in the middle of the saddle, which means right into its deepest point if a saddle is well made and well fitted.

If you slightly tense your vertically held torso – but without becoming at all stiff – your hips will exert pressure on the front of the saddle in the direction you want the horse to go. You constantly try to press your hips forwards towards your two fists, and at the same time, as it were sticking to the saddle, follow the swings of the horse's back. The pressure exerted by the constant bringing forward of your hips amounts to a forward leverage, whereupon the horse goes forwards.

Your thighs should be stretched loosely downwards, with your buttocks resting as fully as possible on the saddle, allowing your knees to stay close in to the saddle. This enables you to clasp the horse better and sit lower. Your knees should be slightly flexed so that your lower legs lie evenly and as flat as possible against the horse's body. The front tip of your boots should hang at about the back edge of the girth; with your low heels slightly springing at each step, your lower legs are held in a state of even, light tension. Without constantly exerting

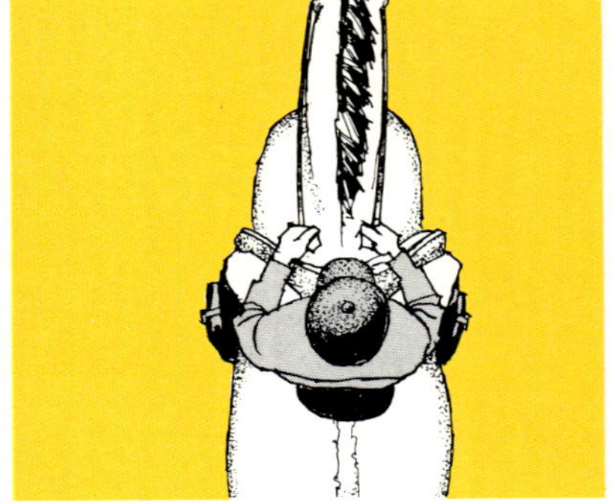

Correct position of the legs, from the side and above

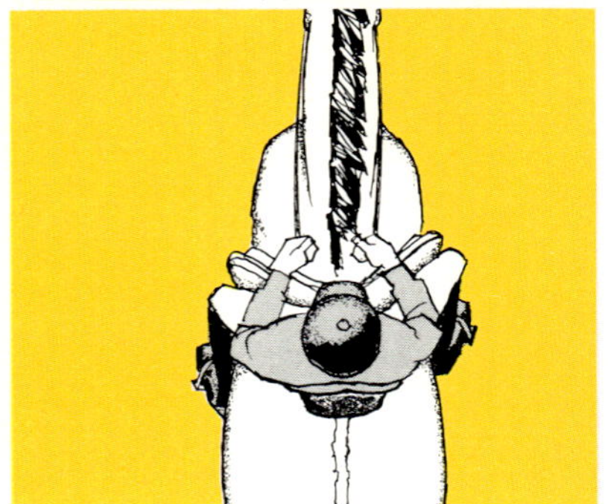

Position of legs when pushing sideways, from the side and above

Perching on a standing horse because the stirrup leather is too long

Obvious in movement too

Chair seat standing still

In movement the fault is even more obvicus

any particular pressure, they should resiliently follow the movement of the horse's body. This doesn't mean they should bounce, but maintain gentle contact with the horse's body. From buttocks to calvés you should be in constant touch with the horse.

The widest part of your foot from the little toe to the ball should rest on the stirrup. If your foot goes too far through the stirrup this usually means that your knee is raised and your lower leg doesn't lie evenly against the horse and increase the tension in your thigh muscle. If your foot doesn't go far enough there is a danger that you will get a stiff ankle.

Your upper body should be held effortlessly straight and your head raised. Your shoulders should be allowed to fall naturally and be pulled slightly backwards. Your upper arms hang down vertically. Your forearm, hand and rein should form one straight line. This straight line governs the correct length of rein and the height of your hand. If the rein becomes too long – which can easily happen, because it can slip thro.igh your hand during riding – your upper arm no longer hangs vertically and the rein aids are no longer given sensitively from the wrist, but can only be given by moving your whole forearm and are correspondingy cruder. If the rein is too short it ɔulls your torso slightly forwards from the vertical.

Right: the correct hand position

Wrong: wrists turned in

Wrong: jutting elbows

Wrong: palms facing down

Your hands should be held palms facing, with the little fingers nearer together than the thumbs so that the palms can be seen. If they are tilted over so that the palms are hidden, or if your wrists are bent inwards, the reins have to be controlled by your forearm instead of your wrist, so the aids are accordingly harsher. It is important not only that your hand is in the correct position but that your wrist isn't braced. Only like this is it possible to have sensitive contact with the horse's mouth.

There is naturally a close connection between the position of your torso, arms and hands, hips, buttocks and thighs.

Faults

- If your torso isn't held effortlessly upright, but you have a hollow back, round shoulders or bottom sticking out, or if you lean too far back or forwards, or if you are guilty of perching (p.66) or a chair seat (p.67), you won't be able to swing your hips forwards, nor manage to stick springily to the saddle and absorb the movement of the horse.

  In all these cases, but especially when you sit too much on the back edge of the saddle (chair seat) or lean too far behind the vertical, your thighs will slip too far forwards.

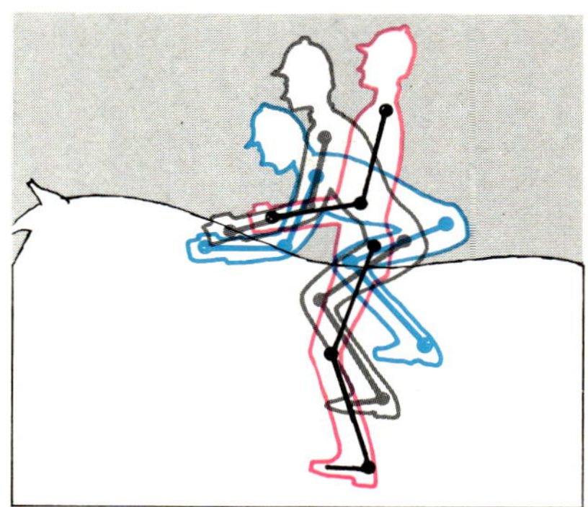

The change in angle of hips, knees and ankles from the dressage seat (red) to the normal light seat position (grey) to the racing seat with extremely short stirrups (blue)

Moreover with a chair seat your centre of gravity will be out of co-ordination with the horse's. This leads to the horse going on the forehand and leaning on the rein or hunching itself up and going over the rein.

If you ride stiffly in the hips and bump up and down in the saddle, this in turn makes your hands jerky, constantly disturbing the horse's mouth.

If you raise your shoulders it prevents your back muscles from relaxing and the small of your back from acting sensitively.

If you turn your feet out and grip too tightly with your lower legs, you will cramp your calf muscles, feel like a knife to the horse, and not be able to swing your hips forwards.

Tip

- You must always work on your shortcomings if you want to correct your seat effectively, because seat faults also inhibit a rider's ability to provide aids. Even practised riders should keep up their seat exercises.

Using the stirrups

Once your seat is relaxed, balanced and secure you can take up the stirrups, without altering the position of your thighs. If your knees and ankles then exert a flexible downwards pressure, the stirrups will without trouble remain under the ball of your foot.

Faults

- Losing the stirrups, caused by drawn-up knees and stiff ankles.
- Standing on the stirrups.
- Pushing the stirrups back to the heel. This could cause an accident.

Tip

- Don't buckle the stirrups too long; exert a springy downward pressure from your knees and ankles; often ride without stirrups.

Correctly positioned stirrup

Wrong: stirrup too far back

Rising at the trot

To relieve a horse, for instance over long trotting stretches in the country, lighten the movement for both the horse and yourself by putting your weight on the horse's back only at every other step, regularly rising from the saddle.

Once you have mastered relaxation and balance you can begin to learn how to rise at the trot. First of all shorten the stirrups slightly, then put them on, lean your upper body forwards, rest your hands either side of the horse's withers, and attempt to lift your seat out of the saddle, taking 80 per cent of your bodyweight on your knees and putting 20 per cent on the stirrups.

Once you have succeeded in holding your seat out of the saddle for a few moments, you can try moving up and down in time with the trot. Before going back to dressage

Rising at the trot: the correct way to rise and sit

exercises in the schooling area, the stirrups must be lengthened again to allow the relevant seat position.

Faults

- Pulling yourself up by the rein.
- Plumping down in the saddle instead of 'taking your seat'.
- Standing up too high.
- Straddling the legs when rising.
- Putting all the weight on the stirrups when rising.

Tips

- Ideally the rising trot should be demonstrated by a good rider – it is much easier to learn by imitation.
- The instructor should count time until the student has got the feel of the movement's rhythm.
- Practise rising without the horse (see p.72, the forward seat).

Changing legs

In the trot, the horse's diagonally opposite legs move in sequence (see p.82) and you should return to the saddle rhythmically in time with one pair of legs' movements. As the direction changes, the legs should accordingly be changed too, which is done by staying down in the saddle for two steps. When riding in open country change legs every couple of hundred metres to burden the horse evenly.

Wrong: pulling oneself up by the rein and then bumping down into the saddle

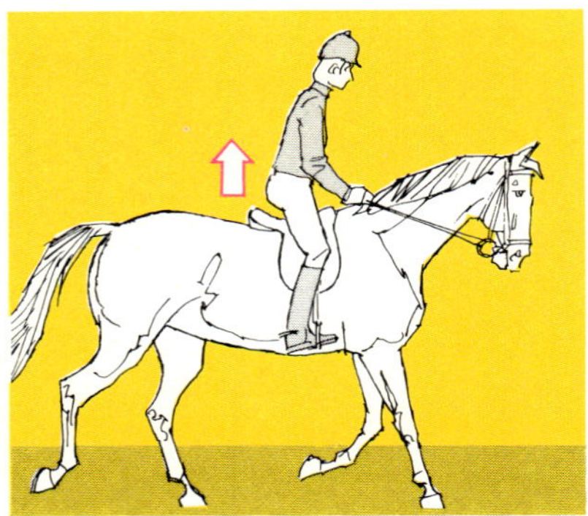

Rising at the trot on the correct diagonally opposite pair of legs (right hand)

The forward seat

Like rising at the trot, the forward seat is designed to make things pleasanter for horse and rider. It relieves the horse's back and enables the rider's centre of gravity to shift during faster movement.

It is essential for you to master the forward seat for cantering in the countryside and for jumping.

Since the forward seat brings into use a different group of muscles, those in your back and thighs, you must learn and practise it in the schooling area quite early on, parallel with dressage training.

Firstly the stirrups must be shortened by three to eight holes, depending on your size. If you are

Rising at the trot on the correct diagonally opposite pair of legs (left hand)

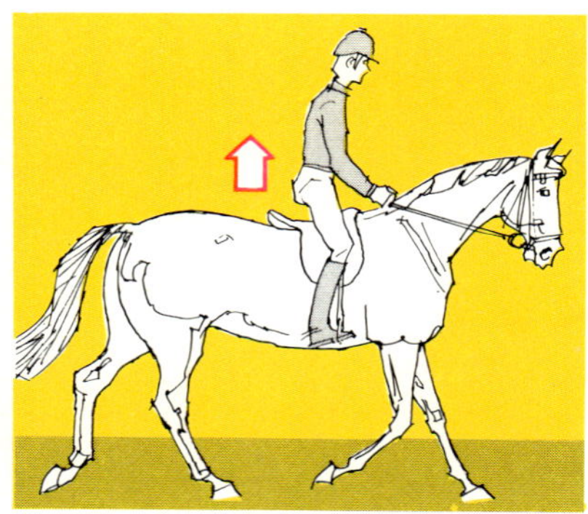

Beginners should be taught to rise at the trot early on to accustom their back and leg muscles to the exertion

small with short legs you can only take them up two or three holes, or else your knees will be brought up too high against the saddle. Riders with very long legs have to bring their seat relatively far backwards to put their joints at the right angles. To make it possible to lift your seat out of the saddle, your torso must shift slightly forwards, meanwhile keeping your spine straight. Your knees take 80 per cent of the weight and 20 per cent rests on the balls of your feet in the stirrups.

Unlike for the dressage seat, for the forward seat your thigh muscles have to be flexed to achieve the knee grip. But as for the dressage seat your ankles exert a springy downward pressure and the stirrups lie under the balls of your feet. You adapt your hip joints, knees and ankles to the movement. This gentle, flexible adaptation to the movement makes things easy for the horse and at the same time has an impulsion effect. Your hands should stay on the horse's neck either side of the withers, so that they can always go forwards towards the horse's mouth. But your hands shouldn't serve you as support; you must be able to sit without their help, and maintain light contact with the horse's mouth.

Along with the forward seat, it is important to learn how to steer a horse by weight alone. You can practise this while riding serpentines across the schooling area using a forward seat.

Faults

- Stirrups too long or pushed back against the heel (which is dangerous).
- Bumping up and down in the saddle.
- Pulling yourself up by the rein.

Tips

- Practise for the forward seat by exercises without the horse: stand with your feet slightly apart, bottom tucked in, hands reaching forwards without holding onto anything, and bounce at the knees, but without humping like a cat.
- Kneel in the saddle.
  Once you have thoroughly mastered the forward seat you will have no difficulty in jumping small obstacles, as you will be able to absorb the movement of the horse's gallop over an obstacle.

Two well-seated riders, with different length legs, at the jump. The appropriate stirrup length gives them the right hip angle

Unmounted exercise for the rising seat

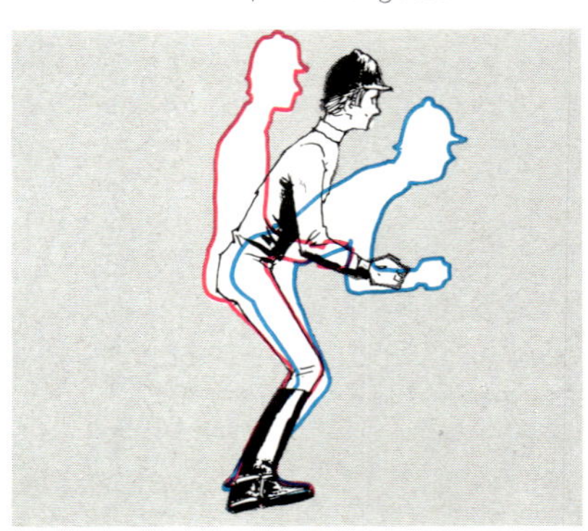

Successful riding depends almost exclusively on feel: the horse can't see the rider but is aware of presence, weight and movement.

Aids are all the physical means of communication between horse and rider which are used to convey the rider's wishes to the horse, as subtly as possible. The better horse and rider are, the less obvious the aids need be.

Aids are therefore not an end in themselves but should just help you make yourself understood to the horse.

Voice

This is a significant complementary aid allowing finer understanding as it does not involve any physical force. Unfortunately vocal encouragement in the saddle is prohibited under many circumstances, being allowed only for young horses or when lunging. All the same, experience demonstrates how much easier it is to restrain a horse with a quiet vocal signal than with a sharp tug – and no rider should be ashamed of making things easier for the horse. You can always speak so quietly that only the horse can hear you.

Whips, spurs and martingales

These are artificial aids, the use of which is controversial.

You have the following means of making the horse understand you: your body weight (back), legs and reins. With these you can make the horse go forwards, stop, move sideways and turn.

First the aids will be described one by one, although they are hardly ever used singly. The following chapter will explain their combination, as they work in practice.

Body weight and back (impulsion)

If you sit correctly on a horse, that is to say your hips can swing with the movement, your good seat is in itself working as an impulsion aid. Your weight evenly distributed over your seatbones in combination with lightly flexed back muscles also have a propulsive effect. If you interrupt your co-ordinated movement, this signals the horse to alter its own movement.

Fault

- Wrongly understood back aids. Instructors often say, 'Ride with your back!' with the result that students tense their torso and lean as far back in the saddle as they can.

Tip
- Imagine you are sitting on a swing and want to start it moving, but without leaning your upper body behind the vertical. It is important to use only the group of muscles right and left of your kidneys.

One-sided weight

This works on a horse in much the same way as when riding a bicycle in a curve. You look in the direction you want to go, your upper body turns the same way and your weight shifts onto your inside seatbone. The horse follows the weight exactly as the bicycle goes into the curve the moment the rider leans that way, even when riding no hands.

Faults

- Don't tilt your hips.
- Don't pull on the inside rein in order to turn, but use your outside leg as an aid (see pp.87 ff.).

Tips
- Practise riding serpentines across the schooling area without a rein, relying only on weight shifting and your outside leg.
- Practise pulling up without a rein by interrupting your co-ordinated movement, so making yourself heavy, and breathing hard in and out.

Legs

Driving

Used both sides your legs support forward movement and engage the hindquarters.

Driving sideways

Pressure on the girth from one leg drives the horse sideways.

Controlling and correcting

The outside leg presses behind the girth when riding curved lines or galloping forwards, for example, so that the horse's hind feet tread in the tracks of the forefeet.

Faults

- Constantly flapping or squeezing legs (also a fundamental seat fault in conjunction with a tense upper body).
- Knees drawn up high.
- Driving with the heel instead of the flat calf.

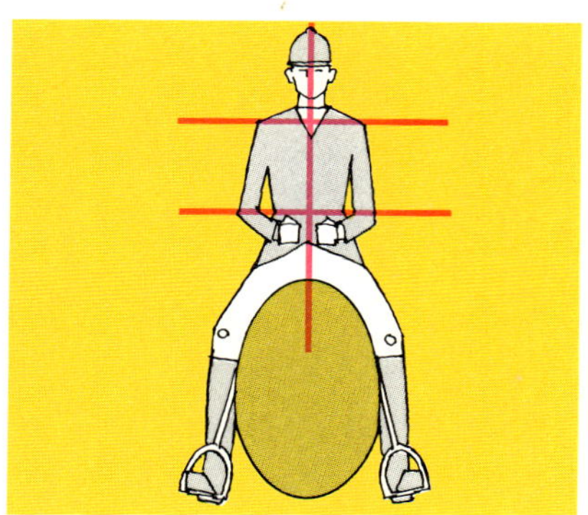

Rider sitting correctly, weight distributed evenly over both seatbones

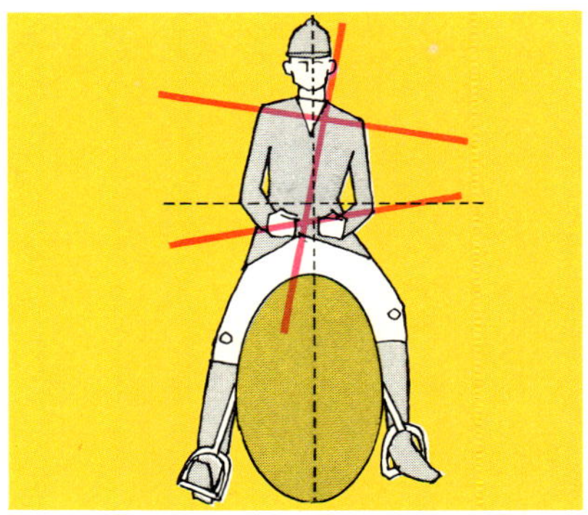

Wrong weight distribution leads to collapsing at the hips

Tip

- Try to feel the horse with an easy, relaxed calf and cling gently to it.

Additional aid

For very lazy horses a stick should be used.

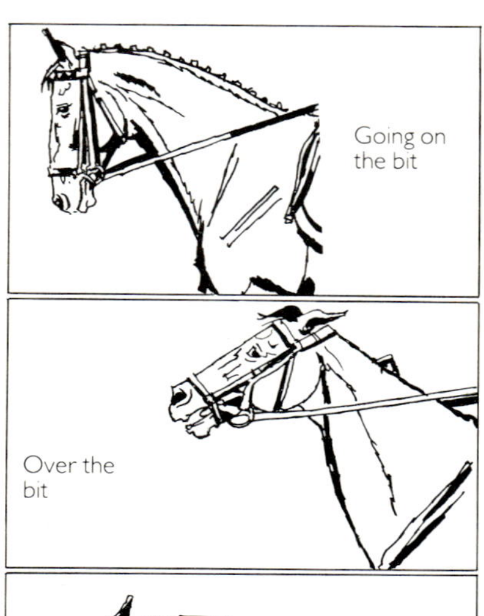

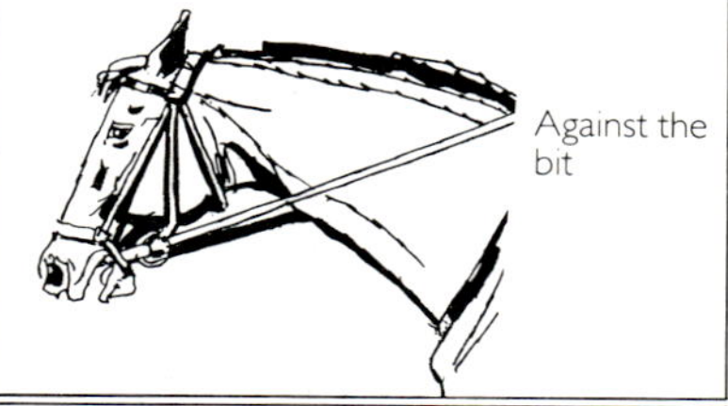

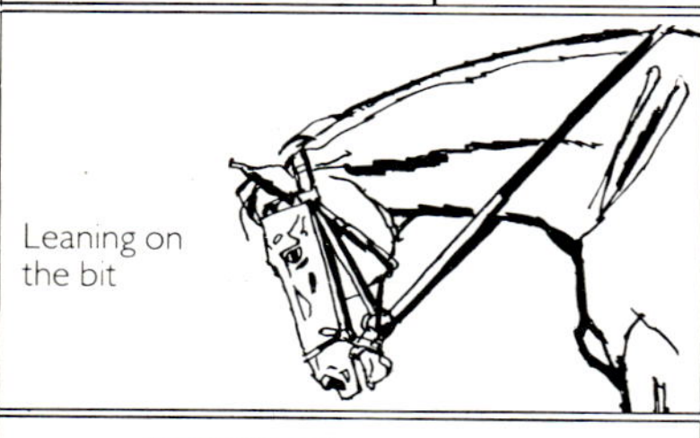

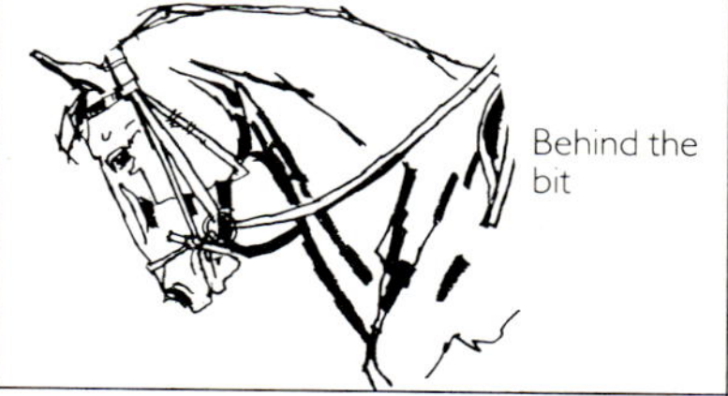

Reins

Reins alone are insufficient to stop a horse or hold it still.

> Reins are used only in conjunction with weight, back and leg control.

The fine synchronisation between hand and horse's mouth is a crucial factor in enabling the horse to feel free despite impulsion.

Yielding hand

This is for increasing tempo, allowing the horse to stretch its neck when out in the country, and jumping. For resting or letting loose relax the rein altogether.

Taking the rein

There is no such thing without giving too! The alternation of take-and-give in combination with the other aids encourages forward movement (see p.79).

Controlling aids

The outside rein works to limit curves much as the outside leg does (see pp.87 ff.).

Faults

- If a horse is held hard by the mouth it will resist the pressure, working more and more against the hand until it finally pulls the rider forwards.
- The hand should never 'saw' on the horse's mouth.
- Yielding the rein shouldn't be mistaken for dropping it entirely.

Tips

- Imagine you are carrying something. Your hand should keep as steady as if you were holding out something breakable.
- Your fingers alone should move, as though squeezing out a sponge.
- The fingers of 'eloquent' hands vibrate.
- It shouldn't only be the hand that yields, but elbows and shoulders too.

Combining the aids

You can only sensibly use the aids in combination, so you should never say a horse is 'leaning on the rein' when you really mean it is 'standing on the aids'.

The combined effect of the aids on the horse produces what we call impulsion. It begins by light contact with the horse's mouth, which is conveyed through the hand, forearm, shoulders and back onto the horse's back. If this circuit is thought of as a chain reaction, then the horse stands 'on the aids' even when the hand moves forwards.

If a horse reacts consistently to the aids and obeys them, professionals speak of 'throughness', meaning that the horse lets the aids be transmitted from its mouth to its back and through to its hind legs.

Here are some exercises to try out and perfect the combined effect of the aids:

- Half-halts and halts
- Making the horse stand still
- Changing the pace (gait)
- Changing the tempo (speed) but not the pace
- Riding turns
- Steering with the legs
- Turning on the forehand
- Backing up

All these exercises are described in detail on the following pages. They have one thing in common, that they demand a lot of concentration from the horse, and it is essential not to overburden it with this type of lesson or to go through them hurriedly. The horse needs plenty of time to translate the rider's signals into movement.

Preparation for any exercise is therefore crucial for its success. If the horse isn't given enough time it will perform in a slovenly or hasty way, or try to get the business over with as quickly as possible in order to evade the clumsy aids.

These lessons should also be done sparingly and alternated with straightforward riding and pace practice on the long rein as a rest from concentration, otherwise the horse will interpret them as punishment and become tense and unhappy.

In fact, riders should ask themselves what they and their horses really can and would like to achieve. The right measure of ambition depends on the pleasure that it gives both of them to approach their set goals, and on the safety factor: riders must always be capable of controlling their horse safely.

These exercises for combining the aids also eventually produce the coincidence of the centres of gravity of horse and rider, in that they make the horse collected and induce it to place its quarters more under the centre of gravity (impulsion) without increasing speed. The horse gradually responds to the aids, relaxes, and allows itself to be more easily steered, provided of course that the rider is skilful and sensitive.

This fine tuning between impulsion and control, however, can't be conveyed by any book. It can only be learnt by feeling and practice.

Halting

Half-halts

Combined with and modified by all the other aids, half-halts are a form of constant communication with the horse, keeping it busy and alert. While the impulsion aids are always dominant, half-halts are effected by lightly closing the hand but not pulling back on the outside rein.

Halts

Halts are a succession of several half-halts that bring the horse from any movement to a complete standstill.

Making the horse stand still

While you sit contained and motionless, the horse must stand quite still. Play lightly with your fingers while your legs feel the horse's body and hinder any side-step.

Faults

- Excessive rein effect.
- Tugging on the rein.
- Weaving or bowing the head from side to side.
- Overwhelming the horse, not allowing it enough time to carry out exercises.

Tips

- Reinforce your physical signals with your voice.
- When reining in from the gallop, count up to three in the rhythm before giving the signal, likewise up to four from the trot.

Changing pace

Aids when walking

Weight Sit relaxed, providing no pressure from the hips.
Legs Close on alternate sides when the corresponding hind leg lifts.

Tip

- If you let your legs dangle, they will fall alternately against the horse's body at the right moment automatically.

Reins Let your hands yield and allow the horse to nod freely.

Aids when trotting on

Weight – back Flex your back muscles on both sides and urge the horse forwards with your hips as though sitting on a swing. Swing from back to front in time with the movement, not letting your upper body lean backwards at all.

Body movement and foot sequence

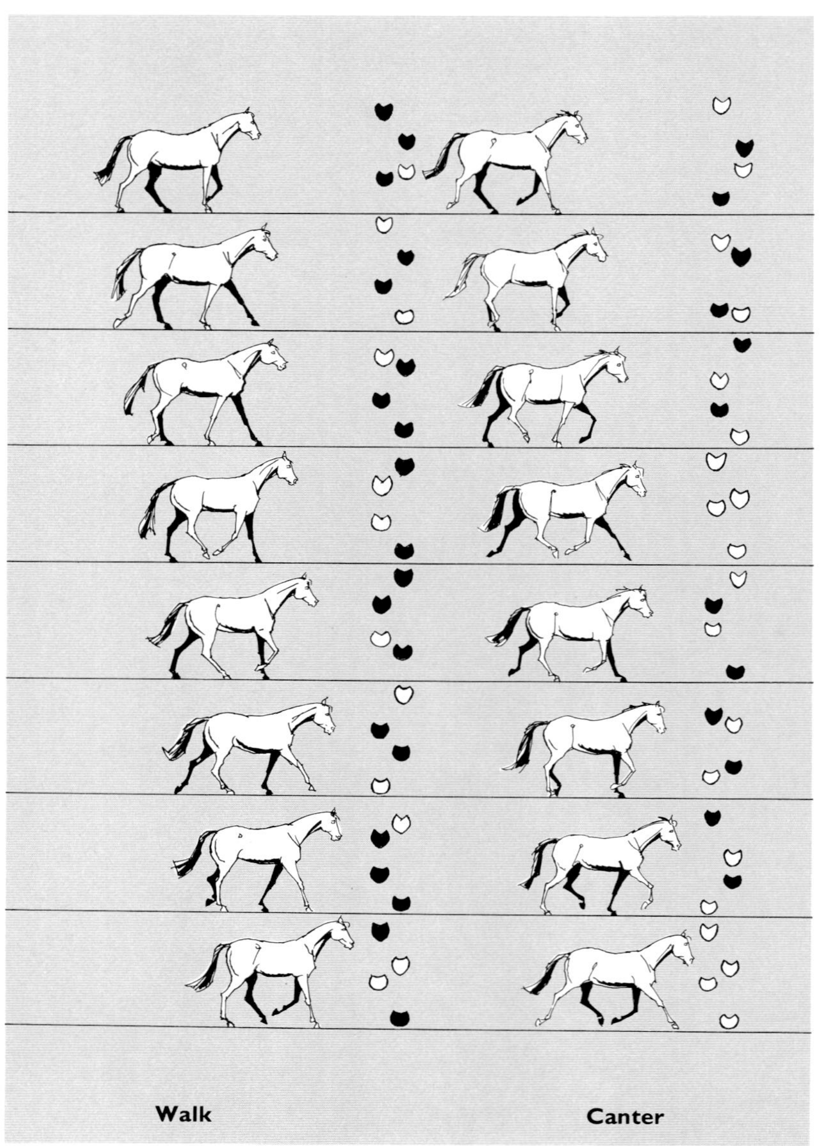

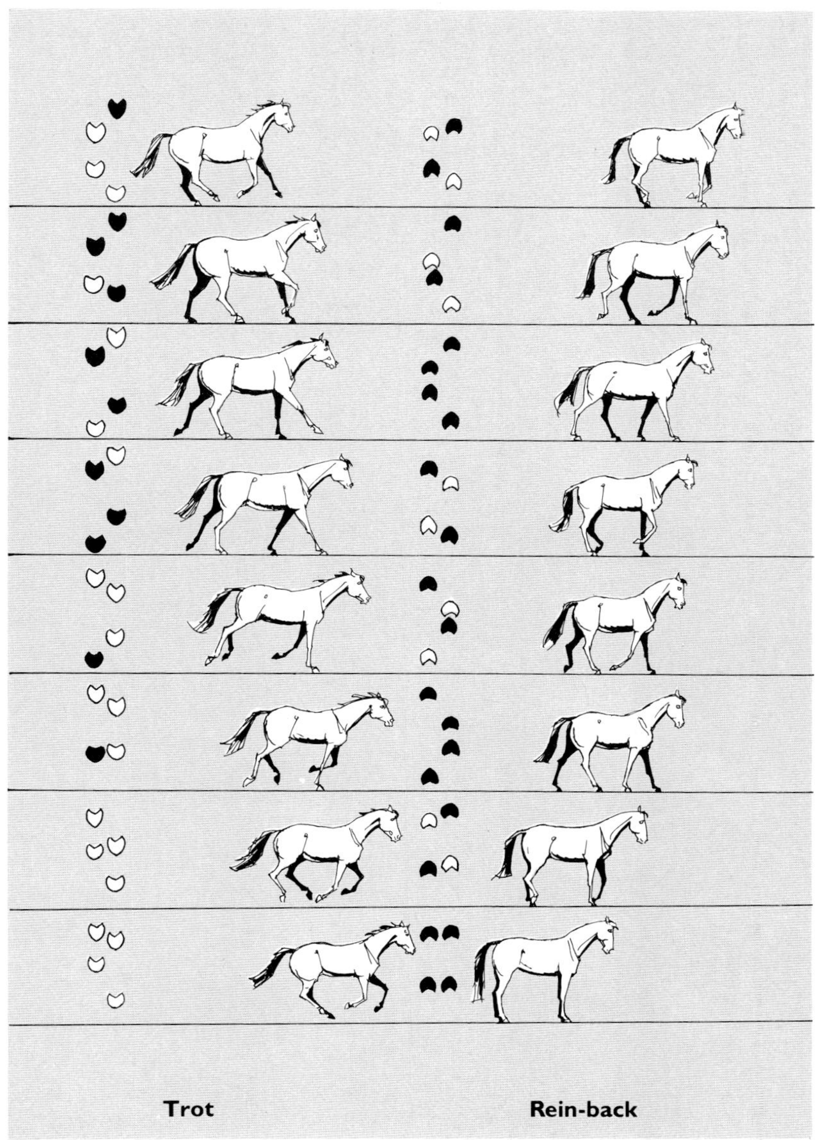
Trot
Rein-back

Legs Close them, push them on.
Reins Yield gently with your hand to allow forward movement.
Voice Click your tongue softly.

Faults

- A monotonously flapping leg not only looks ungainly but becomes habitual for both horse and rider and contributes nothing to either – the horse becomes deadened and the rider's whole body eventually becomes cramped and can no longer enter into the horse's movement.

Tip

- If the horse is deadened and hard to send on, the rider shouldn't try using stronger leg pressure and ever sharper spurs, but rather resort to the aid of a stick. Just a soft, springy flick with it from the wrist should suffice.

Aids for cantering on

The rider's cantering position
Weight Rest on the inside seatbone, with your shoulders back.
Legs Close your inside leg on the girth while your controlling outside leg lies behind the girth.
Reins Do half-halts on the outside, until it is time for the horse to break into a canter, then reach forward with your inside hand to give rein to the canter stride.

The horse's cantering position
Your position should angle the horse slightly towards the inside, which will make it easier for it to canter on correctly.
Cantering on Impulsion from your inside leg produces the canter. The inside rein yields.
Seat for the canter You must remain firm and still in the saddle.

Faults

- Jogging seat
- Too much urging movement in the upper body.

Tip

- Don't slither or try to 'polish' the saddle, but remember you have a joint just below the waist, and you should only go along with the cantering movement with your hips, not with your whole upper body.

Changing tempo

If the horse goes into the canter incorrectly, you can see this from the shoulders; it leads with the outside pair of legs instead of the inside. A rider who has learnt to feel what is going on will notice that the horse has 'struck off on the wrong leg'.

Tips

- Canter along curved lines, then the horse will have the correct position.
- Provide the impulsion to canter on when the inside hind leg lifts.
- Always go into a canter from a walk or a calm trot.

Tempo increase from working walk (above) to brisk walk (below)

Walk = working walk increasing to a brisk walk

Trot = easy trot increasing to a working trot

Canter = working canter increasing to gallop

Changing tempo but not pace

At this stage in training it is of prime importance for horse and rider to change tempo within the same pace, without wishing to place emphasis on the correct performance of, say, a working trot or a brisk trot, which doesn't fall within the scope of this book but concerns the dressage rider.

Let us therefore content ourselves with an average working tempo for all paces, developing an increased tempo from this.

Above: Working trot
Below: Extended trot

Above: Working canter
Below: Gallop

A working tempo is an active, rhythmic tempo suited to the horse in question, neither hurrying nor lagging.

When increasing the pace, all movements should cover more ground but be neither more hurried nor more rapid.

To decrease the tempo, use several give-and-take hand movements to reach the regular, flowing working tempo.

Hint Create increased impulsion with your back and legs, following the forward movement of the horse's head with your hands, without altering your posture.

Faults

- Urging so hard as to lose the beat.
- Leaning the body backwards – a bad fault.

Turns

Riding a turn

We distinguish between riding straight and riding on a curve. In both cases the horse's hind feet should always cover the prints left by the forefeet.

(On the straight, horses not yet completely trained can be seen to walk crooked or bent. This is natural and inborn to animals and humans alike. By equal bending on both sides the horse can, in the course of training, be taught to hold itself straight.)

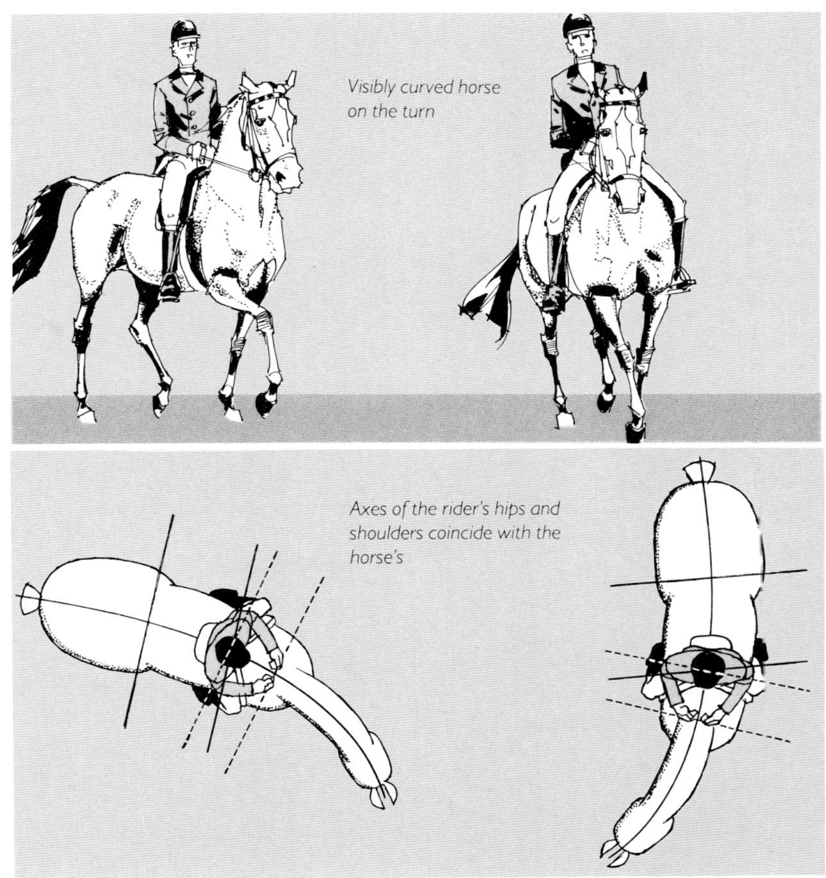

When turning, the horse's entire spinal column must follow the line of the curve. When this is the case the quarters still cover the tracks of the forehand, and the rider can see the inside eye and the glistening rim of the inside nostril.

Begin a turn by looking in the direction you want to go. This brings your shoulders into the correct position and shifts your weight onto the inside seatbone. The turn is controlled by your outside leg and the outside rein. Your inside leg makes sure that the horse's inside hind leg treads well underneath, while the inside rein yields.

The outside rein in a turn

The outside, controlling rein is so extremely important that we would like to discuss it in detail in this chapter.

Nearly all riders set out with the false assumption that you turn a horse by pulling on the inside rein and make it stand still by give-and-take movements on the inside.

Children on ponies and all beginners have to grasp that the outside rein and the inside leg must be used in conjunction: the inside leg pushes on to the outside rein, and the inside rein yields.

When walking, trotting, and later cantering, all riding students should learn to feel how easily a horse lets itself be turned when they give with the inside hand instead of pulling.

If you want to change direction during a turn, then of course you have to 'sit round' and allow the horse a few steps' grace to adjust itself.

Faults

- Pulling the horse round by the inside rein.
- Forgetting to signal with the legs.
- Putting the weight wrongly on the outside instead of the inside.

Tip

- Practise turns using only weight shifting and your outside leg (and don't tilt your hips).

Leg yielding

Leg yielding serves the following purposes

- It is obedience practice for the horse.
- You learn to push one leg on effectively.
- You learn to use your inside leg to send the horse onto the outside rein.

Method

The horse is slightly bent round the pushing leg and against the direction of movement, and walks step by step sideways, which puts it at an angle of about 45° to the fence.

Aids For example, let the left leg steer. It is sensible to begin the exercise from the second corner of a short side, as the horse will already be in the correct position there. The forehand now steps onto the second track as if you wanted to turn away out of the corner. Then the left leg pushes on the girth, making the horse step sideways and sending it onto the outside (right) controlling rein and leg. The outside (right) leg now lies a handsbreadth behind the girth and exerts control to prevent the horse going back onto the track or 'slipping' sideways too quickly.

The rider's weight rests on the

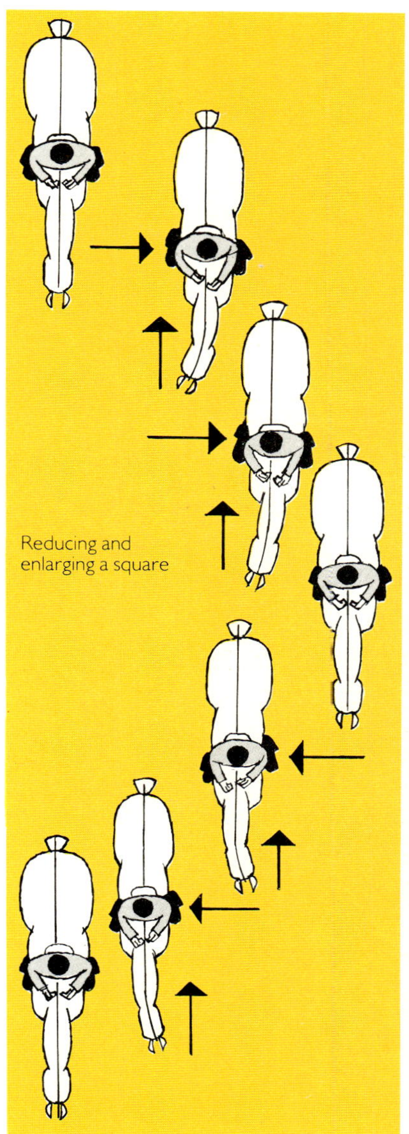
Reducing and enlarging a square

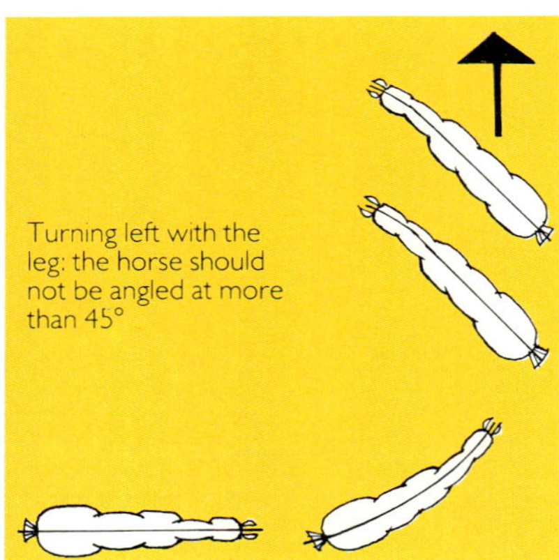
Turning left with the leg: the horse should not be angled at more than 45°

inside (left) seatbone. The right hand steers the horse in conjunction with the right leg, while the left, in conjunction with the left leg, keeps the horse steadily angled slightly to the left.

Faults

- Angling the horse at more than 45°.
- Pulling only the horse's neck round, its forehand staying on the track.
- Making hand signals too strong.
- The outside, controlling leg fails, and the horse doesn't step across correctly.
- Pushing the horse too hard, so that it shuffles or stumbles sideways instead of stepping calmly.
- Tilting your hips.
- Pulling up your pushing leg (and heel).

Tips

- If the horse is insensitive and doesn't respond to the leg, you can resort to the use of a stick.
- Steer with your legs as follows: ride straight down the centre line, then from the centre point onwards steer with your right (or left) leg and ride sideways onto the track, just as when reducing and enlarging a square. This will naturally accentuate the foward movement – the horse will move instead of shuffling, as unfortunately often happens when steering with the leg against the fence.
- The inside hand must continually yield, as the horse should stay on the outside rein.

Important

- Do this exercise only in part sections; direct, straightforward riding should always take precedence.
- Try to avoid steering horses with the leg when their heads are to the fence, as this is not a good exercise for them!

Turning on the forehand

Although turning on (or about) the forehand is described in every riding manual and demanded by many dressage exercises, its only real purpose is to convey to the rider how pushing sideways with the leg should feel. For the horse it makes even less sense, for it is done too much on one spot and often places too much load on the forehand.

Method

The hind quarters should walk round the forehand, for which the horse is bent round the pushing leg, exactly as in leg yielding (see p.89).

Aids As in leg yielding, turning on the forehand is done only from a standstill.

Fault

- Usually the horse's head is pulled towards the fence and the quarters driven round the forehand as fast as possible. All too often this makes horses tread on their own feet, with the result that they either decide to hurry of their own accord to get away from the inexpertly given signals, or will only do the exercise reluctantly.

Turning right about the forehand, shown in three stages

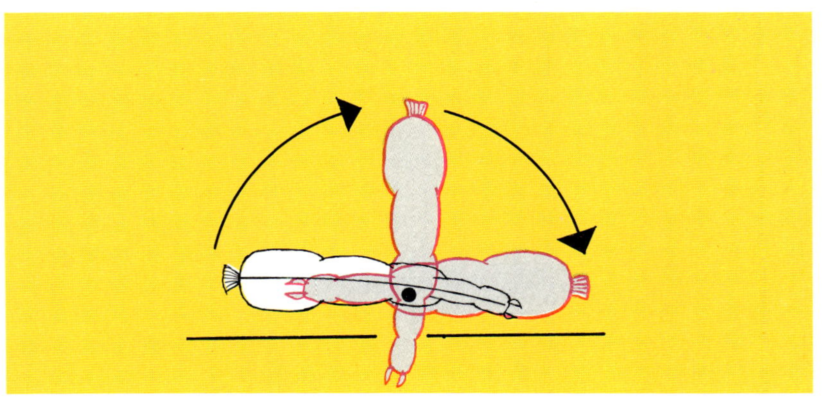

Tips

- It is more sensible to learn the action of pushing sideways with the leg by starting at the centre point (X) of the schooling area and pushing the horse sideways towards the track (see p.90).
- If you absolutely have to practise turning on the forehand, then please do it only on the second track and slowly, one step at a time!

Reining back

This exercise is a test of how well a horse obeys the aids, because walking backwards is an unnatural and unpleasant form of movement for horses.

Method

A horse should never have to be forced to walk backwards (it is really not yet flexible enough), but should willingly tread backwards in a diagonal foot sequence, not being allowed to stumble nor shuffle nor stagger sideways. The rider must be capable of controlling each separate step – and up to four steps are enough!

Aids Starting from a standstill, reining back is initiated by forward impulsion, converted however into walking backwards by a firm yet vibrating hand. At the same time take your weight off the horse's back, gently, without falling forwards. Your legs should lie equal, a handsbreadth behind the girth, both gently pushing and controlling. In this way they urge movement by gently pushing and at the same time determine a straight walk backwards (controlling).

Faults

- Pulling backwards (sawing)
- Leaning the upper body backwards
- The horse stumbling backwards
- The horse walking crooked.

Tips

- Don't practise reining back until the horse is relaxed to the aids.
- Don't practise reining back too often, but content yourself with a few steps, and take care to give exceptionally sensitive signals so that the horse doesn't interpret the exercise as punishment.
- Reward the horse after the exercise.
- Practise reining back along the fence for a start; this helps to keep straight.
- If it doesn't work, get someone on the ground to help you, and use voice commands.

Riding in the countryside

Riding in the countryside should be a pleasant and relaxing occasion for both horse and rider. Before a first outing you should make sure of certain requirements and that all participants understand the procedures to follow

- The most important is a calm, footsure horse.
- It is essential that you have trotted and galloped in the schooling area free from the lunge and are capable of controlling your horse.
- The first outing should if possible not pass through stretches of traffic, which might make novice riders insecure and nervous.
- Outings should be in small groups of not more than four to six riders.
- An experienced rider should take the lead and another bring up the rear.
- If possible ride two by two, which reassures horses and riders.
- Maintain at least two horselengths distance between riders.
- Start the outing at a walk.
- Remember to tighten the girth.
- Trot for long stretches as a loosening up phase, rising at the trot changing legs.
- Return to walk every so often.
- Ride these walking intervals on a loose rein so that the horses can relax and look around – this also improves the walk.

A rider lifting her weight off the horse's back to help it climb up or down a steep slope

More and more riders are realising how relaxing it is to idle through beautiful landscape on horseback for several hours. Without the pressure of competitive performance you can be at one with your horse and feel the full effect of nature's beauty

- Choose a gallop stretch that leads away from the stable; horses have a fine homing sense and they could be tempted to rush homewards.
- Don't gallop on too narrow a path, which could cause an accident.
- When galloping uphill leave the tempo and duration of the gallop to the horse.
- Horses enjoy taking short steep slopes at a gallop; here it is essential for the rider to hold onto the neck, not the rein.
- A gallop must be followed by walking on a long rein.
- Descend slopes at a walk, sitting upright. Horses should be led down longer slopes.
- If you suddenly need to rein in, calm the horse with your voice; don't snatch at the reins or kick.
- The duration and tempo of a ride should be determined by the ability and disposition of horse and rider.
- End the ride at a walk on a long rein.
- The horse must go into the stable dry.

Points to watch

- Avoid asphalt, stony roads and deep sand; sand is as bad for the sinews as asphalt for the bones and gravel for the soles. Never ride faster than a walk on these surfaces.
- When riding out be aware of the horse's breathing. Too often riders enjoy a gallop so much that they forget the horse needs to pause for rest.
- It is a lovely experience just to take your horse out for a walk and let it graze in a woodland glade. This is certainly more natural for a horse than diving into a country tavern.
- Riders should not only watch out for and greet people who are rambling through the country on foot, but try to avoid their footpaths.
- Riders who force walkers to leap into the bushes are unchivalrous!
- It is equally unchivalrous, and also dangerous, to gallop past other riders. You should meet and overtake cautiously at a walk, which also gives you the opportunity to exchange greetings.
- You must not ride over cultivated fields nor over meadows and pastures, nor protected areas, nor footpaths and cycleways.
- After the outing, attend to the horse: sponge down its back, nostrils, muzzle and anus. Look for wounds while showering down and hoof cleaning. In cool weather lead your horse around for a few minutes.

Riding in traffic

In traffic ride two by two, as close together as possible, or in single file in narrow streets

- Safety is paramount. Traffic-shy horses have no business on the road, but should practise in the yard at home.

Normal traffic regulations apply to riders too. They should behave just like a motor vehicle or cyclist.

- Riding in town traffic isn't allowed.
- Outside built-up areas riding on the pavement or the road is a matter that must be left to the rider's judgment. You should only ride on a pavement when there are no pedestrians about.
- Riders in a group should all cross the road together, if necessary warning traffic with hand signals.
- Never ride more than two abreast, the less confident horse on the left. It is better to ride in single file.
- If leading a horse, do so from its right, and use the lefthand side of the road keeping the led horse between you and the fence.
- In the dark a horse must wear reflector fetlock bands and a rider a light on the right stirrup, showing white in front and red behind.
- Vehicle drivers are obliged to watch out for animals. Deliberate hooting, accelerating or noisy gear-changing are inadmissible.

After sunset both horse and rider must wear fluorescent bands and carry a light

Jumping

The horse, as we have established, is a herd animal, and from an early age foals with their mothers will naturally get over all sorts of small obstacles. It makes sense to use these natural propensities of horses in training to jump.

It is no accident that the best event riders come from England, where the riders on sure-footed horses almost incidentally gain their first jumping experience over small natural obstacles in the countryside.

With the help of this natural method, jumping can be learnt in the course of normally flowing movement, without horse and rider having to plan each jump as a major operation.

A jump of whatever height or breadth is only an extended gallop stride, and if you like you can adapt yourself to the airborne phase with a raised seat, staying catlike and flexible on the horse, as long as you have mastered rising in the saddle.

Capitalising on horses' herding instincts, practise jumping with a number of horses, led by an experienced horse and rider whom others will follow.

Horses usually jump natural obstacles in the countryside readily and safely

A condition for this, however, is that the horses know the method and don't break away, so that a distance of at least two lengths can be maintained.

For their part, riders need to have enough faith in the method, their horses and not least themselves, that anxiety doesn't suddenly make them grab the reins and upset the horses' natural flow of movement.

It is very important to bear in mind that horses will readily take off even before small obstacles if they are only given the chance.

A horse enjoys jumping from a flowing gallop much more than if it is held back to parade and then allowed to take off. (Only a few riders ever have the ability to do as the great experts and make the take-off right for the horse.)

This natural method of letting the horse jump and learning to go with it is a surer way of building up mutual confidence. You should entrust yourself to the horse, and the horse should be able to trust you not to put it off.

As the horse doesn't have to jump alone, but follows the lead horse, it jumps with confidence and fluency and it will never occur to it to refuse. In this way it is much easier for beginners to acquire the feel of the natural jumping movement sequence, than on horses which regularly swerve past, baulk or break away.

As a rider you will take for granted the horse jumping readily. As the horse takes off, reach your hands as far forwards as the horse needs to extend, less for small jumps, more for higher and broader ones. Leaning forwards too suddenly confuses the horse. You should maintain a light contact with the horse's mouth. You must always be capable of reining the horse in after the jump – but vocal commands are better than tugging at the reins.

Faults

- Staying behind the movement
- Gripping the reins too hard

Tips

- A neck strap will help a beginner to develop a steady, low hand.
- In certain cases very small jumps may be mastered at the trot with a rising seat.

When horse and rider are sufficiently confident, they can of course take each obstacle either as leader or by themselves.

Horses are always especially watchful and cautious before obstacles constructed of poles. This rider is giving the horse the freedom it needs and blending perfectly with its movement

Hunting

The spectacle of a hunting field may enthral observers, but for horses and riders the prospect of galloping freely in lovely surroundings represents a well-deserved reward for gruelling hours of work, sweating away in the schooling area. Safe from the critical eyes of instructors or colleagues, riders can give rein to their own knowledge, courage and skill.

To get the most out of hunting, however, horse and rider need to be adequately prepared. A good hunting horse must be well broken-in, responsive to the rider, a good jumper, good tempered, healthy and with stamina – qualities that can't be expected immediately, but must be systematically built up and earned.

With the right training and preparation, practically any riding horse can go on a simple hunt. Younger horses are schooled in company with others, or are ridden in fields for young horses. It is obviously foolish to ride exclusively in the schooling area and then take part in a hunt unprepared. The horses will be excited by the many unfamiliar and new surroundings, become impetuous and get in the way of other riders and their horses.

The same basic principles apply to hunting as to hacking.

The saddlery must be checked and the stirrups buckled two holes shorter. During the hunt an even tempo must be ridden, set by the Master. All riding and jumping must be straight ahead, so that no-one obstructs a neighbour.

High-spirited horses should be ridden at the sides of the field, so that they always have the opportunity to turn or swerve sideways. Continuous hanging back behind the field and then galloping up again not only makes the rider's own horse nervous and violent, but also all the other four-legged participants and spoils the rider's enjoyment too.

The fences are wide, so they can be taken by several horses at once. If a horse refuses, its rider mustn't simply turn aside as is the custom in a single event, but must first make sure that doing so won't hinder a fellow rider. Riding too fast up to a jump or across a field is dangerous, and can all too easily result in damage to the horse in front, such as ball-tread.

Hunting demands extreme discipline and courtesy, and hunters must always respect agricultural activity.

In England hunts ride over many different types of land e.g. moorland, marsh, farmland and parkland. Each hunt has its own designated area and is responsible for any damage done to that land.

A hunt with hounds, following the pack, is one of the most exhilarating experiences a rider can have.

The behaviour of each hunter in the field can influence the outcome of the hunt. Here is a little advice:

- Be aware of other riders in the hunting field.
- Ride a kicking horse at the back of the field, never in the middle.
- Crossing a hunting field endangers oncoming riders and is to be avoided.
- Never jump behind another horse unless at a safe distance.
- Good jumpers should be ridden at the head of the hunting field, young and insecure horses at the rear.
- When a place has been chosen for jumping, if you stay nearby, following riders can prepare for it.
- Be considerate to anyone riding a young horse.
- Don't gallop too close behind or in front of them past an obstacle.
- Lively horses should be ridden at the sides of the field, where a wide turn can be carried out unhindered if necessary.
- If a horse comes to a halt before a fence, don't veer to one side until the way is clear.
- If anyone falls the next rider should of course go to their assistance.
- It is forbidden to overtake the Master.
- The wearing of correct habit and a well-secured riding hat is obligatory.
- Be particularly careful of onlookers.
- After a stop it is advisable to lead heavily sweating horses and not leave them in a draught.

Hunting is one way to experience nature, for every landscape has its particular charm. We should all contribute to the protection and maintenance of this fine sport for the pleasure of others and ourselves.

Transporting horses

Preparing for transport

It is better to be overcautious and pack the horse up well with rugs and bandages than run the risk of its hurting itself or catching cold.

To make the journey more agreeable for the horse, every horsebox or trailer should be provided with a hay-net.

Horses will need fresh air on a journey, but draughts are dangerous. On a night journey, leave a light on in the box or trailer if you can.

Loading

Loading must be done unhurriedly and carefully. Horses will load more willingly if the ramp isn't too steep and it is light inside the box or trailer. If a horse is still reluctant, 'wings' can be placed either side of the ramp, or long reins held taut, and the animal can be enticed with titbits. The simplest way is to load another horse first.

When leading a horse in, never look straight at it.

These two horses are obviously enjoying their journey

Avoid any sort of fuss. The only thing achieved by hitting and shouting will be that the horse learns to associate loading with pain and anxiety and will be even more intractable next time.

Loading should be done without a rush. Particularly difficult horses may be fed in the vehicle occasionally beforehand.

Unloading

Before the ramp is let down, the horse must be untied.

Unloading requires the same calm as loading, or else the horse may get excited and jump down sideways off the ramp.

Lead it round a little afterwards to stretch its legs.

Transport-shy horses

Many horses allow themselves to be transported better alone in a double horsebox, because they suffer claustrophobia in a single one. Others, however, are nervous alone and calmer when they have company. Only time will tell.

A horse well wrapped up for the journey with mesh anti-sweat sheet, brushing boots and tail guard

Driving a horsebox or trailer

You should drive as you would with a baby or elderly grandparent in a car, moving and stopping smoothly and sensitively, braking in good time before curves and avoiding all noisy gear-changing or backing.

Children and horses

The earlier riding is learnt, the better, but small children belong strictly on small horses.

As a rule, pony-riding can be started at the age of seven or eight. Earlier, all the business with horses is physically too demanding. In any case a good introduction to horse management, and good riding instruction or show jumping training which the child can grasp, must be provided.

It is important to learn the correct way to saddle and bridle a pony. Often far too large bits are used and the saddle sits badly. It is sensible and nothing to be ashamed of to use a breast strap and crupper to hold the saddle firm on the pony's round back.

Parents must be quite clear as to their child's capabilities. Children often overestimate their own strength and fail to judge something they have done wrong. Here the parents can help to teach – but remember that children nearly always imitate their parents' behaviour. Don't be over-ambitious. Children should learn by riding and by handling horses. They should cultivate responsibility and companionship, not jealousy, unhealthy ambition and selfishness. In this, a horse can be an educative influence that the child must adapt to.

Ponies are often much more obstinate than horses. In contrast to nearly all horses, a pony is aware of its full body-strength. This can teach children one of two things, either to use their wits and skill to persuade the pony to do what it has to, or – and this would be a pity – to try and impose their wills with roughness and force.

The pony must therefore be presented to children in the proper light; the child should see it neither as a toy nor a pet, but must be constantly steered by intelligent adults into the correct behaviour.

It is ideal to take a child out at first on a leading rein, holding the rein in your right hand and keeping your horse and the child's pony abreast. This is a fairly safe way to teach children correct hacking behaviour. The great advantage is the opportunity for example and imitation; children are known to learn mainly by imitation.

Although children and horses generally get on well together, you should take elementary safety measures

The pony as comrade in play and sport

Riding provides good motivation in every respect for many children. The horse obliges them to accept the advice of adults – and difficult children often prove easier to handle at home when they themselves have to handle horses.

Wise parents will delay buying children ponies of their own until they have really shown that they are capable of accepting responsibility for it and have learned to care for and ride it sensibly.

Even taking part in gymkhanas should not become the source of jealousy and ambition but, on the contrary, should promote and reinforce group awareness and comradeship.

Trekking

All riders will want to set themselves a minimum and a maximum target. For recreational riders it is a worthwhile plan to have a holiday on a farm with your family and the fully involved horse. If you have a fit, mature horse used to both countryside and traffic, and know about its behaviour and management, have mastered the rising trot and achieved a degree of confidence about riding in the countryside, then you can certainly think about a riding holiday. This is the best opportunity for the whole family to get on terms of trust with the horse, not just as riders, but particularly in looking after it. It would be ideal to plan a holiday with two families and several horses – but please not unless you all understand each other and are compatible riders.

Suitable locations

The first consideration, of course, is whether the chosen spot is right for horses; the soft ground of moorlands and downs, for instance, is better for a horse's legs than stony, mountainous terrain, which requires a more robust animal. Most travel agents will have particulars of suitable holiday spots and horse trekking.

Preparing the horse

Of course the horse must be prepared for the holiday, particularly if it has been ridden mostly in the schooling area. A horse is trained for the country just as people are for jogging, being at first allowed to gallop short stretches and then gradually longer ones at a free and easy tempo.

Planning the holiday

Even on holiday your time should be sensibly organised so as to preserve the horse's strength and the riders' enjoyment. It takes a few days for everyone to get used to each other, but after about a week you can plan a day-outing, then at the end of the holiday your enthusiasm and energy may flag a little. You must definitely stick to an overall programme, so that non-riding members of the family can take part too and no quarrels arise, for example coming along on a bicycle, jogging, taking turns on the horse, swimming with the horse, having a paper-chase or, if several members of the family ride, you could try an 'orientation relay race'. For this, similar to a motor-rally, establish places along the route where the horses change riders. This should prevent jealousy from those who are only mounted on bicycles! You can also have a duty rota for such jobs as cleaning the horses, shopping, picnic organising and so on. Picnics with the

horse are particular fun, quite apart from the fact that they are an ideal chance for a rest.

Equipment

Naturally all the accompanying hands must be responsible for some of the equipment themselves – which should be no problem with the help of the bicycles.

Saddlebags can be attached to hold the following items:

- Pocket first-aid kit (headache tablets, stomach trouble medicine, lip salve, bruise spray, healing ointment, antiseptic powder, insect spray).
- Dressings and bandages, maps, washing things, rainwear, pocket-knife, picnic utensils (horsefood when trekking) etc.
- Aluminium sheeting in case of accidents that have caused shock. The victim will not lose heat if wrapped in the sheeting. It also protects from damp while perhaps having to wait a long time for removal.
- Waterproof riding coat, preferably with a hood.
- Light, windproof jacket (but not ski-clothing!).
- Crash helmet or reinforced riding hat.
- Special unbreakable spectacle cases with some device for latching them on safely.

For the horse

- Head collar (a nylon one will slip into a pocket), tether, mesh anti-sweat sheet, perhaps a night-rug, hoof pick, wire, pliers, wound spray, fodder, pocket knife.
- In summer a sponge soaked in anti-fly spray, which can be kept in a plastic bag, is vital.

Holiday treats

A horse that has been kept exclusively in a stable can be allowed to spend hours in fields during holidays. However, for such a horse grazing can be so unfamiliar that it has to get used to it gradually. The best times for this are the morning and evening hours, for in high summer horses suffer a lot from heat and insects.

The early morning is also the most beautiful time for a ride. Even if it is a treat to sleep in during the holidays, you should once in a while enjoy the experience of watching the sunrise with a horse in the open countryside.

A night ride is also a very special experience. Horses see very well in the dark – and you don't have to be particularly romantic to enjoy the occasional ride by moonlight.

Horses love the snow, just like dogs and children. The tedious problem of compacted snow in the hooves can be alleviated with a hoof leather kit or, better still, a rubber insert called a hoof grip (ask your supplier). Snow doesn't clog unshod hooves.

If you can't avoid icy places, studs should be screwed into the horseshoes, and you should let the horse pick its own way.

- A horse is neither a pack-ass nor a galloping machine.
- During breaks, unsaddle the horse and put on its head collar and mesh anti-sweat sheet, feed and water it and let it graze.
- It is essential to look after your horse's hooves.
- Ask your blacksmith to tell you beforehand what to do if a shoe comes off.
- Before riding through woods, ask permission.
- One more thing: riding over long stretches is tiring not only for the horse but for the rider too, and if you become stiff you ride less carefully. It is therefore advisable, as well as a pleasure, now and again to go on foot.

Considerations

Apart from the cost involved, owning a horse means accepting a great responsibility. Anyone thinking of buying their own horse should be a good, experienced rider, have plenty of time available and be in a position to offer the horse suitable accommodation (a large stable, the best attention, pasture, and the company of other horses) in addition to good facilities for riding practice (open-air and indoor riding areas and ground).

There should always be somebody who can look after the horse if you yourself are prevented; it is sheer cruelty to leave a horse standing in a stable all day long. Even when it can go out to grass it needs someone who can see to it at least once a day.

You must be able to make reliable long-term arrangements; makeshift provisions are bound to create problems.

You must be absolutely clear what you want the horse for: Do you just want to go for country rides? Do you want a family horse? Or perhaps a show jumper?

The horse you choose must suit you not only in size and temperament, but also in ridability. There is no point expecting too much of yourself. If you have insufficient experience in horse training it is senseless to buy a young horse or to believe you can correct a badly schooled one. Too good a horse will quickly throw a bad rider over its head, unless you have the opportunity to take regular instruction and ensure that the horse is prepared.

If you genuinely fulfil these conditions for owning a horse, then you must allow yourself adequate time to find the right animal for you.

Judging a horse for the layman

As a non-professional you can nevertheless find the right horse for your needs if you let yourself be guided by your observations and sound common sense. You won't need to canvass all sorts of expert opinions, nor be vulnerable to convincing patter from the would-be vendor.

Someone riding simply for pleasure and exercise doesn't need a beautiful specimen of horseflesh, but rather a fit, good-natured horse which is in sympathy with you at first sight. The first impression is always the most important, and the decisive factor is the horse's good temperament.

First of all look at the horse you are interested in in the stable. As soon as you open the door it should approach trustingly with pricked-up ears and sniff at you. It should have a friendly, positive personality, just as you would expect from a human being with whom you want to strike up an acquaintance, for it is essential that a relationship should be established between horse and rider.

Next you should ask for the horse to be given something to eat and drink, to make sure that it has not been made limp and apparently docile for lack of water and food.

The next thing to do is to put a head collar on the horse, lead it out of the loose box and make a preliminary trial grooming – possibly to the surprise of the vendor! For the private buyer who wants a horse to join the family, a trial grooming will tell you a lot. It gives you your first close contact with the horse; you can determine whether it is calm, lets its hooves be lifted, has healthy skin and sound limbs, and whether it appeals to you or not – also whether you appeal to it!

After that you should saddle and bridle it, preferably yourself, and watch it being ridden about in the arena and in the open.

Finally you should try it out yourself in the stable yard, the riding area, the countryside and the road. It is essential to feel good on the horse, be able to sit comfortably and have confidence.

If everything is to your satisfaction you should ask to get a vet's confirmation of its soundness, then return a couple of days later before signing the contract and go through the whole viewing procedure again, for, like us, horses are not in the same mood every day.

Gently trotting the horse will give you some idea about whether

- The horse will move rhythmically and relaxed at all paces.
- It will accept the bit quietly, without sticking out its tongue, stretching its jaws or champing its teeth. If it does this it will produce a quantity of white foam at both sides of its mouth – the sign of a soft mouth.
- The horse carries its tail free and quiet, and it swings loosely from side to side as it moves. A tail sticking out, pressed down or constantly swishing indicates physical or mental tension. Swishing the tail, unless to ward off flies, denotes resistance to the rider.

A beautifully harmonious airborne phase over a jump

It is also a good idea to observe the horse in the stable over a long period beforehand, to see if it has any stable vices, for these are very hard to correct and can become unpleasant in the long run.

After all, even between people and animals love can occur at first sight, causing many small faults to be overlooked. Buying a horse is a bit like getting married – you only realise later what you have taken on – except that it is easier to separate from a horse! But even horses can't be changed like clothes.

Difficulties stemming from temperament are very hard to eradicate. You have to learn to live with them, or look for a horse that suits your own temperament better.

Anyone who is having trouble with a horse ought to consider whether they really do have a problem horse or whether the fault lies with the rider.

Properly understood problems can be put right, and after all, no horse and no person is faultless.

Tips for horse owners

- Provide good, regular feeding.
- Check drinking water.
- Groom your horse daily.
- Exercise it daily.
- Check the saddlery and look after it.
- Check stable rugs; when the horse is casting its coat, remove loose hair from the underside daily.
- Hang up a salt-lick in the loose box.
- Ensure that the stable is well ventilated.
- De-worm your mount regularly.
- In case of sickness, call the vet; don't try to play the doctor yourself.
- After illness, especially after lameness or cough, allow adequate convalescence and after-care.
- Get insured.
- If a horse has to be destroyed, call the vet.

The sick horse

Anyone who is with horses daily and watches them will gradually learn to recognise the signs of poor well-being and health in good time, not only when an illness has reached its peak.

Eating habits and the condition of urine and droppings have to be regularly checked, as they tell the expert a lot.

A run in fields even in winter is part of the healthy rearing of horses

A horse suffering from a cough enjoys inhaling soothing steam

Signs of a healthy horse

- Alertness, interest
- Lively ear-play
- Clear, shining eyes
- Dry, pale pink nostrils
- Sweet, odourless breath
- Gleaming, smooth coat
- Soft, elastic skin
- Cool, trim, dry legs
- Evenly warm ears, neck and rump
- Normal thirst
- Good appetite, vigorous chewing
- Pale yellow, cloudy urine
- Staling every 2½ to 3 hours
- Firm, even, brownish droppings

Symptoms	**Diagnoses**
• Spitting out while chewing (not caused by environmental disturbance)	Tooth trouble, pain in the mouth or brain disturbance
• Very careful chewing, letting chewed fodder fall out of the mouth	Decayed or broken teeth
• Eating grass, hay and straw but refusing oats	Tooth trouble or digestive disturbance
• Rejecting fodder and eating soiled litter	Mineral deficiency or stomach and bowel catarrh
• Red or dark brown urine	Feverish illness, stiff back
• Pale droppings	Liver pains, bowel catarrh
• Small, hard droppings	Disturbed bowel movement
• Soft faeces with much undigested seed	Too hasty feeding without thorough chewing
• Pulpy faeces	Chill, diarrhoea, poisoning
• Slimy faeces	Stomach and bowel catarrh
• Reddish, bloody faeces	Intestinal bleeding

Problems with horses

The horse has a set of behaviour patterns that enhance its survival ability in the wild. Shying, bolting and napping, for example, are conditioned by the horse's characteristics as a creature of flight.

These behaviour patterns persist in domestication and under a rider because they are innate. They are rather unpleasant for a rider and can even be dangerous, but if you want to control them you must view them with understanding, not see them as stupidity or obstinacy when they become a problem for you.

Other difficulties arise from bad riding and wrong handling. A horse is sensitive and reacts in its own manner to a rider's faults. This is not recalcitrance, but only an attempt to avoid getting hurt. Riders should seek the fault in themselves before blaming the horse. Problems that have been correctly recognised can as a rule be solved, but because riding involves two living creatures it often takes time, patience and above all understanding.

Resistance against people is usually nothing but reaction to wrong treatment, for the horse is essentially good tempered and submissive – precisely because it is a herd animal. When handled well and sympathetically it will accept humans as superior fellow creatures and respect them accordingly.

When in any difficulty there are three things to bear in mind:

- The horse is fearful by nature and only feels happy when with its own kind.
- People must use their intelligence to understand the animals and treat them appropriately.
- The horse can only be controlled by trust in people together with habit and practice.

Shying

Shying is a sudden swerve aside which creates a chance of survival for the flight animal. The horse's highly developed sense organs give it very early warning of dangers, well before they become apparent to us. It can feel the vibration of the road under a lorry, for example, before it comes into view.

For the rider, however, shying is not very pleasant, particularly as it often happens so suddenly. For this very reason you shouldn't allow yourself to get tense and worked up at every possible suspicion of danger, for often the horse will just be upset by this and made aware of things that might not have concerned it at all.

With the sudden fright riders often react impetuously, becoming aggressive with the horse to work off their own feelings, and trying to force it past the 'dangerous' object. This unfortunately only increases the horse's fear.

It is wiser to use your human intelligence and take the line of least resistance than attempt pointless trials of strength that only anger both horse and rider and contribute nothing to either's training. In fact the horse shies neither out of stupidity nor to annoy. The only stupid thing is for the rider to react unthinkingly – after all, when bringing up children we succeed in teaching them sensibly with the help of our superior intelligence.

The simplest solution is to make use of the herd instinct and let a calm horse go in front. If you are alone, attempt to soothe it by speaking calmly and patting it and letting it sniff the obstacle. You can even try taking it past backwards or with averted head, otherwise there is no shame in dismounting and leading it past. All this is more use than dragging and thrashing, because the animal must be given confidence.

If the horse shies in the schooling area at something that it will have to pass many times in the course of the lesson, for example some object on the fence, the first thing to do is pass by giving it as wide a berth as possible. After a few rounds it will have forgotten the frightening object. This is a much simpler, more effective method than pulling and tugging because 'the nag's making such a stupid fuss!'

Shying

The more trust the horse has in people, the more variety it gets in its daily work, and the more it is let out to pasture and in the countryside, then the less it will shy. But a horse which experiences nothing but the path between loose box and schooling area is more easily frightened.

Bolting

This is innate fleeing behaviour, which, like shying, is vital for the survival of the free-roaming horse and has a contagious effect on its fellows.

It is induced by fear

- of external objects (such as a railway)
- of the rider (continually bumping in the saddle for example).

If a horse bolts it must on no account be further upset, perhaps by shouting; on the contrary, it is essential to speak soothingly to it, making give-and-take movements with a low hand on one side. If the ground is suitable, you can try to steer it round in a circle.

A horse with a tendency to bolt should be ridden only at a walk or a trot; cantering, whether in the schooling area or out in the country, should only be practised on the lunge.

Sharp bridling or deliberate over-riding to tire a horse out will never bring success; it will come as the horse gets used to being ridden and learns to trust the rider's hand.

Napping

Clinging to its fellows, known as napping, is part of a horse's natural behaviour, a feature of its herd instinct. For the rider, however, it can sometimes be a problem, but here again battling is useless, as the horse is acting instinctively.

It is better to accustom a horse gradually to going alone, starting, for instance, by taking two horses out of

the group. After a while the companion returns to the group and you attempt to gallop off alone.

It is important to instil a horse with trust in the rider, whom it will then eventually accept as a fellow. This sometimes happens more quickly if the horse is frequently led.

Plunging

Plunging and bucking are faults only from the rider's point of view. For the horse they can be an expression of joy and high spirits. And why shouldn't a horse rejoice in its own way once in a while? A good rider will adopt the light seat and allow the horse to prance about, absorbing the movement.

Unpractised riders should regularly let their horse run free so that it can plunge all it wants. Every horse needs this sensation of freedom.

Plunging

Misbehaviour caused by riders

Head shaking

This always indicates a horse's discomfort. The cause may be flies, a badly fitted bridle (tight head strap), saddle pressure, a rider's hard and restless hand, or back pain from a bumping rider.

These external causes can easily be remedied. If the rider is at fault, the head shaking may be corrected by energetic forward riding on a long rein. The rider ought to notice the head shaking as soon as it starts and create more impulsion by back and leg signals while riding on.

Martingales cure the symptoms but not the cause.

Head shaking

Head shaking by young horses should be ignored. It usually disappears spontaneously as the animal gets used to being ridden and bearing a rider's weight.

Going over the rein, leaning on the rein, ducking the head and tongue faults

None of these is misbehaviour in the true sense, only the horse's reaction to force and pain.

A horse that is ridden calmly, without too much emphasis on 'going at the rein', will never develop such habits at all.

They all originate from inadequate or faulty training or too hard and wrongly understood impulsion. A rider's hard, dead hand always creates a hard mouth in a horse. A sensitive hand that never weaves about but keeps the fingers flexible (like squeezing out a sponge) will be gratefully accepted by the horse.

Correctives

Ride forwards, sitting down firmly in the saddle, providing impulsion of course, but without letting the horse feel your hand as a prop.

Here again martingales do no more than allay the symptoms, but not the causes.

Bucking

Rearing

This is the horse's most unpleasant misbehaviour, and it too is the consequence of a rider's fault. Mostly, too hard a hand is the cause. A horse rears because it is the quickest way to get free from the pain in its mouth, for on a rearing horse a rider is fairly powerless.

As soon as a horse begins to rear you must yield and ride forwards, if possible turning and riding in a circle.

When the horse rears, you must bend your upper body forwards and hold on with your arms round the horse's neck. It is fatal to hang onto the reins as this can make the horse somersault.

The correction of rearing horses must really be left to an expert!

Rearing

Biting

Aggressive behaviour of horses towards people

Biting and kicking

Biting and kicking are defensive reactions against people. They are never innate behaviour but the consequence of improper treatment.

Horses only bite and kick when they can no longer flee, and it means they just want to get away from people.

It requires much patience, understanding and persistence to wean a horse out of this behaviour. You must restore its trust and be particularly considerate and kind to it.

If a horse bites it should at once be given a tap on the nose so that it knows it shouldn't. There is no point in punishing too late or too hard, or in being resentful, for the horse itself is not resentful, but goes by experience. If it is punished too severely it loses still more trust and will reject people still more strongly.

Insurance

The owner of a riding horse is held to be unconditionally responsible for all damage caused by his horse to a third party. A liability insurance is an automatic must for every horse owner. If a horse falls that is no disgrace, but unfortunately not every fall is without penalty. Members of riding clubs are generally insured against riding accidents when taking part in club events, but not when they are riding out privately. Private accident insurance is therefore always advisable.

Damage suffered by the horse can be covered by part insurance or by a comprehensive animal life insurance.

There are three kinds of insurance:

Third party insurance for damage that the horse may cause to third parties.

In both town and country, horses that never shy are the best life insurance

Accident insurance for damage to the insured party.

Animal life insurance for damage suffered by the horse.

Every riding horse owner should take out these insurances. On top of these there is the possibility of insuring both horses and horsebox or trailer against theft. Naturally the animal insurance companies have the widest practice, while others have specialised in particular types of insurance, and offer special competition-horse insurance, liability insurance for owners of riding horses, and riders' accident insurance. There is even a special insurance for small breeds of horse.